SpringerBriefs in Psychology

SpringerBriefs in Theoretical Advances in Psychology

Series editors

Jaan Valsiner, Aalborg University, Aalborg, Denmark
Carlos Cornejo, Escuela de Psicologia, Pontificia Universidad Católica
de Chile, Santiago, MACUL, Chile

More information about this series at http://www.springer.com/series/14346

Koji Komatsu

Meaning-Making for Living

The Emergence of the Presentational Self
in Children's Everyday Dialogues

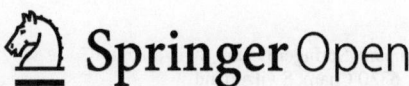

Koji Komatsu
Faculty of Education
Osaka Kyoiku University
Kashiwara, Osaka, Japan

ISSN 2192-8363   ISSN 2192-8371   (electronic)
SpringerBriefs in Psychology
ISSN 2511-395X   ISSN 2511-3968   (electronic)
SpringerBriefs in Theoretical Advances in Psychology
ISBN 978-3-030-19925-8   ISBN 978-3-030-19926-5   (eBook)
https://doi.org/10.1007/978-3-030-19926-5

This book is an open access publication.

This Springer imprint is published by the registered company Springer Nature Switzerland AG
The registered company address is: Gewerbestrasse 11, 6330 Cham, Switzerland

Series Editor's Preface

"Shall I compare thee to a summer's day?"[1]

It could be said that William Shakespeare should be remembered as a prominent psychologist, as the beauty of his sonnets brings poetry into the realm of our investigation tools in human psychology. It is the affective subtlety of poetic tools that give promise for our scientific investigations. The theory of Presentational Self outlined in this book has everything to do with poetry—even if there is no direct poetry in the meticulous coverage of everyday interaction events that Koji Komatsu presents. Yet I would claim that poetic expression is the ultimate example of the Presentational Self—something in the poet's current relation with the ambience triggers, and that something "bursts out" from the interior infinities of the person into the interpersonal realm of a poem, a song, a dance, or a painting. The roots of such outbursts are in the person <> environment continuous, relating within the flow of experience. So also are its outcomes.

Poetry is returning to the science of cultural psychology in the twenty-first century in powerful ways. It becomes the root for new methodology (Lehmann et al. 2017) as well as becomes discerned in the researchers' efforts to make sense of deep experiences in human lives (Lehmann and Valsiner 2017). Yet poetry is mysterious—the identity of the "thee" in Shakespeare's sonnet is never revealed. It remains invisible—yet its invisibility provides guidance for the affective adventure to experience the sonnet. The affective field evoked in the reader of the sonnet emerges and proliferates as the description of the "summer's day" continues. We realize that this description is not of a real summer day, but of the interior feelings of the author whose readers have resonated with the sentiment over the past four centuries. The poet's feelings become expressed as relations with the Other (the "thee")—the Self is a *liminal organizational form* on the pathway from the internal infinity of the person toward the external infinity of the environment. In that location—"in between"—the Presentational Self as outlined in this book has a parallel with the notion of Educational Self (Marsico and Tateo 2018). The latter starts from the

---

[1] First line of William Shakespeare's (1609) Sonnet 18 (The Poems of Shakespeare 1832, p. 153)

v

institutional forms meant to create tensions on the border of the person <> environment system. The former begins from the simplest acts of reflecting upon the world—listing which peers are in the same play as the child or reporting one's experiences traversing through the world. The Presentational Self is active all the time and everywhere.

Koji Komatsu is not a poet but a meticulous observer of events in everyday life, looking foremost at the processes of relating between parents and children. Seemingly nothing interesting happens there—a parent questions the child about the mundane school day or schoolchildren write about events of various kinds. There are periodic reunions of families, school groups, and so on. Life seems ordinary—yet Komatsu brings us to appreciate the extraordinary in the ordinary world. In these repetitive acts triggered by the "Other," one can observe the externalization from the interior of the *psyche*, taking the form of a generalized kind on the border with the *Umwelt*. The notion of the Self is set up in the peripheral arena—*in-between* the person and the environment. This theoretical innovation is perfectly legitimate—yet it is in dire contradiction with the common language notion of self as something internally hidden within a person. Common sense guides us to locate the self somewhere in the interior of the human psyche. Finding it on the border is counterintuitive, yet for theoretical progress inevitable. Why?

It is the *open systemic* feature of all human existence—complete dependence of our lives upon exchange relationships with our environments—that locates important phenomena of human living in the periphery—on the border. It is here where the presentation happens: the person tells others with whom one did something together, saw in some setting, or experienced at some time somewhere. All folkloric transfer of non-written myth stories of a society from one generation to the next is based on such presentation processes. In such settings, both the story teller and the listeners are building up their own ways of relating to the world. Presentational Self is the generalized system of the production of signs that organizes the ongoing social relation with the environment in relation with other human beings, acting as a tool for development of the meaning-making system of the person. It is a *Bildung* device—by reflecting upon experiences, the person builds up one's ways of being as a cultural meaning-maker.

There are other centrally relevant functional systems that are located in the periphery. The closest analogues in the rest of our organismic existence to Presentational Self are the immune system and the system of biological and semiotic borders that concentrate on the skin. Both the immune system and the skin-related psychological functions are also located in the periphery. Obviously, the function of the immune system is to capture the viruses that are attacking the body and neutralize them. This has to happen at the entrance point—where the virus encounters the organism—and is hence located on the border of the organism. That border is given by the basic membrane that envelopes the body: the skin. The skin operates as the border area for bidirectional transfer of biological substances and—in the recently developed Semiotic Skin Theory (Nedergaard 2016, and forthcoming)—operates as the peripheral arena for the personally relevant meaning construction. All three peripheral (yet centrally relevant) systems operate through generalizations—the immediate here-and-now event becomes generalized and hence usable in the future. The immune system needs to arrive at the generic decision—"is this incoming agent part of my organism or is it alien?" If the latter, it needs to be blocked based on the previous experience (i.e., vaccination).

The Presentational Self is a generalizing vehicle to bring relevant understanding of the world out of the most ordinary experiences in daily lives. Through the constant return to the presentation of most ordinary (and recurrent) events, different hyper-generalized feelings are created by the Presentational Self. Presentational Self is the psychological mechanism for hyper-generalization, leading to our creation of values and personal life philosophies (Zittoun et al. 2013). The demonstrations of how it functions in childhood years that the reader of this book encounters can be extrapolated to the whole human life course.

What is Komatsu's secret, the "invisible" in the Presentational Self exposition by the author? He is a careful observer of the ordinary life events—yet with a deep general philosophical credo of understanding that goes beyond each of the immediate setting that he describes. His efforts presume the whole being constructed through the seemingly repetitive elements that trigger the building of the whole. Another well-known Japanese thinker, Kinji Imanishi, has explained it concisely:

> I do not see the world as a chaotic or random thing in which members are like chance passengers on a ship, but as having a certain structure or order and each of its members having a function. Although the various things in the world have an independent existence, they are all in fact in some kind of relationship. (Imanishi 2002, p. 1)

The Presentational Self theory as outlined in this book is precisely a story of searching what kind of relationship is created by mundane questioning of events in daily lives. The function of such ordinary acts is in their qualities of uniting the concrete with the abstract (hyper-generalized reference to *myself* as *Self*). The structure implied is assumed to be a multilevel organizational form that adjusts to the given circumstances of the ordinary discourse. It is as if our lives in their daily ordinariness are parts of a lifelong drama of self-construction where the Presentational Self guides us to make sense of ourselves—yet it does not become an equivalent of an entity ("thing"). And this is perhaps the most important lesson for Occidental psychologies to learn from the tender, invisible, but persistent Oriental traditions of understanding the World: what allows us to develop are processes deeply invisible, the kinds that operate upon very visible ordinary acts in our lives.

Aalborg, Denmark   Jaan Valsiner
October 2018

References

Imanishi, K. (2002). *A Japanese view of nature: The world of living things*. London: Routledge (original Japanese publication in 1941).

Lehmann, O.V. & Valsiner, J. (Eds) (2017). *Deep Experiencing: Dialogues within the self.* Cham: Springer.

Lehmann, O,V., Chaudhary, N., Bastos, A.C. & Abbey, E. (Eds.) (2017). *Poetry and imagined worlds.*. Cham: Palgrave/Springer.

Marsico, G., & Tateo, L. (Eds.) (2018). *The emergence of self in educational contexts*. Cham: Springer.

Nedergaard, J.I. (2016). Theory of semiotic skin: Making sense of the flux on the border. *Culture & Psychology, 22*(3) 387-403.

Nedergaad, J. (in preparation). *Semiotic skin theory*, New York: Springer Briefs.

The Poems of William Shakespeare (1832). London: William Pickering.

Zittoun, T., Valsiner, J., Vedeler, D., Salgado, J., Gonçalves, M. & Ferring, D. (2013). *Melodies of living*. Cambridge: Cambridge University Press.

Acknowledgments

Many of the ideas presented in this book were elaborated through the discussions with the members of "Kitchen seminar" at Clark University and Aalborg University, led by Prof. Jaan Valsiner who is also the series editor of this volume. Two commentators, Mogens Jensen and Tania Zittoun, also gave me advice when I examine what I wrote formerly. I am grateful to the current and former colleagues at Osaka Kyoiku University for their support while I worked on this research project.

This work was supported by JSPS KAKENHI Grant Number JP16K04301, JP16KK0056. Linguistic proofreading was made by Patrick O'Shea.

Contents

About the Author

Koji Komatsu is an associate professor of psychology at Osaka Kyoiku University. The inquiry into the process of children's meaning construction and the emergence of their selves presented in this book is the result of his long-standing interest in human development in the society. In addition to this subject, he inquires into several topics concerning culture and mind that also describe our meaning construction in mundane lives.

Chapter 1
Who Can Know *My Self*? A New Look into Psychological Inquiries Into the Self

Mina: And where [we] visited long ago, when [I was] a baby?
Mother: When [you were] a baby, Umeno Park.
Mina: Yeah, right. Was Mina cute as a baby?
Mother: So cute.

(From a conversation between Mina and her mother recorded during a car ride. Mina is 4 years and 6 months old. See Excerpt 1.1 and Chap. 3 for details of data collection and transcription.)

In our everyday lives, we keep constructing the *meaning* of our experiences and ourselves. Daily conversation, as we see above, is one example. In the episode above, a young girl, Mina, and her mother are reminiscing about their visit to a park. They discuss Mina in the past, with the young girl suggesting to her mother that she, Mina, was a cute baby. It is a suggestion concerning who Mina was in the past, and it is achieved through a series of exchanges about their past. We can observe here the construction of Mina's self-representation through an interaction. However, does the self *only* emerge in such straightforward descriptions of ourselves? Considering the succession of exchanges in the conversation we experience, the self is not what appears suddenly when we mention ourselves but rather what is constantly under construction throughout the process, and the description of ourselves is only a part of this process.

Regarding this fundamental understanding about the self as it appears in the interactions in which we participate, in this monograph I strive to formulate a new perspective on the self with support from theories that indicate the nature of our minds and *meaning construction*. In this theoretical framework, children's selves are *not* the results of forced reflection as posed by researchers. Direct questions to children or adults do not lead to reporting about the self—rather, these questions reveal their thinking about what the self might be. On the other hand, this is the point at which the "psychologists' fallacy" described by James (1890) occurs—we often confuse what we understand and what we are going to describe as functions of the minds of study participants.

Instead, we can observe the self as it emerges when children attempt to reconstruct and present their experiences and their expectations for the future.

© The Author(s) 2019
K. Komatsu, *Meaning-Making for Living*, SpringerBriefs in Psychology,
https://doi.org/10.1007/978-3-030-19926-5_1

This is also the self *we,* researchers or observers, find out investigating the inter-actions in which children participate, because the researchers' positions for interpreting children's conduct must not be hidden or ignored. With this primary orientation, I pay attention to the dynamicity of how children's selves emerge, which cannot be grasped by approaches based on the epistemological position of most psychological research.

Further, when we look at interaction in natural settings, another point of inquiry is how and why it occurs in our lives. For this question, I attempt to inquire into various real-life situations where some *dialectic tensions* work to promote development, both at micro and macro levels. Thus, the discussion hereafter is an endeavor to understand the self in the midst of the real world, not in the virtual field consisting of researchers' intentions.

We Construct Meaning to Live on: Facing the Future

Although we do not care about mundane activities in our very ordinary lives and soon forget what we have done, we are always recognizing what we experience and finding the next way to behave. When I meet one of my friends, for example, I am recognizing a variety of experiences on site to construct the interaction. Of course, the name of my friend comes to me when I notice him in the crowd, and I search for my first words in consideration of the last time we met. In the interaction that follows, I will consider many things about him, his family, or experiences we shared in the past, for example, to facilitate conversation with him. This is not limited to our encounters with others. Valsiner (2007) gives the example of saying to oneself "I like this" when observing a painting (p. 29). It is also an example of how we find out the meaning of our affective experiences and control our attitudes towards them. Thus, we relate to ourselves through signs, as semiotic cultural psychology has indicated (Valsiner, 2007). From this point of departure, I inquire throughout this monograph into the process of how signs function in the self-construction processes.

A variety of signs with social and cultural backgrounds are at work in these processes. Our language constitutes the semiotic processes, mainly as *symbols*, but *iconic* signs—typically an image of an object and an *index* that "enforces our atten-tion to an object" (Valsiner, 2007, p. 42)—are also working in our minds. However, the most important point here is not such a categorized understanding of signs, as they often work in hybrid ways (Valsiner, 2007), but their function to create mean-ing for the future, if they are used to describe experiences in the past. Valsiner (2007) discussed this function as follows:

> Each meaning, or sign, that is in use during the infinitely small time "window" we conveniently call "the present," is a semiotic mediating device that extends from the past to the possible, anticipated (but not knowable) future. The promoter role of these signs is a feed-forward function: they set up the range of possible meaning boundaries for the unforeseeable, yet anticipated, future experiences with the world. *The person is constantly creating meaning ahead of the time* when it might be needed (…) (p. 58)

Many researchers of psychology have focused on the meaning we construct retrospectively concerning objectively important events from the macro perspective, through established summary categorizations of life experiences. For example, the categories "meaning of my job," "a serious illness," and "unforgettable" or "traumatic" experiences are all categories of some outcome of self-reflection. They ask participants to narrate their experiences and the processes are considered the meaning construction. These discussions also introduce the concept of the self both as an agent in constructing meaning and as the representation constructed through the process.

What we find in our ordinary lives is different from such a specific, long-term way of understanding but it has the same characteristics; that is, we meet something, find the meaning of it through the use of signs to achieve distance from the experience, and then act in relation to that meaning. The excerpt of conversation I introduced at the beginning of this chapter also exemplifies this process. It is a very short interchange and does not describe the events in detail. Additionally, it is not a meaning construction concerning the here and now but rather recounts what happened in the past. However, in the flow of interaction, the child and the mother are actively creating an image of themselves and their relationship, and this work functions for the next moment of interaction, as we will see in the analysis of the episodes of conversation. Thus, who we are in relationships and in environments becomes clear in such a process of semiotically mediated meaning construction, and the following discussion is premised on this presupposition concerning our interactions and ourselves.

How Interaction Develops to Describe a Child: A Foundation of the Emerging Self

The make-up of the interaction in which we find children's meaning construction is different from the one we find in psychological research. In ordinary research, we are used to *asking* study participants questions expecting some statements about themselves; that is, queries in questionnaires or probes in semi-structured interviews that function as the starting point for some clarification concerning themselves. Conversely, the meaning construction we observe in real life develops in a series of interactions. For example, the episode of conversation I presented at the beginning of this chapter is extracted from a longitudinal recording of the conversation. As I describe in the forthcoming chapter, recordings were made during their car ride, mainly while returning home from the nursery Mina attended (*hoikuen*[1] in Japanese),

---

[1] In Japan, when the recordings shown in this monograph were made, there were two types of institutions for young children before elementary school: *yochien* (translated as kindergarten) and *hoikuen* (or *hoikusho*) (translated as nursery or child care center). I use the Japanese expressions. On the basis of family background and local government policy, the majority of children were enrolled in either of these institutions. Currently, the Japanese government is promoting gradual integration of these two types of institution, introducing a third type of institution that combines the roles of the two preceding systems.

and the transcript of the recorded interaction clarifies that this exchange is preceded by the child Mina spotting a bus stopping on the street near her home (Excerpt 1.1).[2]

Excerpt 1.1 (original Japanese is in Komatsu (2002))

 1 Mi: Ah, bus!
 2 Mo: Yeah, it's a bus.
 3 Mi: In Mina's home.
 4 Mo: Yes … Let's turn in the corner over there. (Yes) It's not Mina's home, (1 s) cause [it's] a road. (1 s).
 5 Mi: Isn't it Mina's home? (1 s).
 6 Mo: Not [our] home, is it?
 7 Mi: [It is] near Mina's home, isn't it? Why [is it] stopping here?
 8 Mo: Yeah, cause the road is wider there, (Yes) (1 s) there's maybe someone getting off [the bus there].
 9 Mi: Yeah so [I think].
10 Mo: [They] went to a trip. (1 s) Going out somewhere.
11 Mi: Trip means going somewhere. (3 s) xx [Inaudible].
12 Mo: A large-sized bus. (1 s) With the same pattern as the bus [they] hired at hoikuen. (1 s) [Do you] remember? Mina.
13 Mi: [I] remember, the zoo and the playland were connected.
14 Mo: Um, yeah, yeah, it was Musashi Zoo Park… Oh no, sorry, Kitano Zoo. (Yes) Where [we] visited this year? (Yes) Kitano Zoo. [I'm] sorry. (1 s).
15 Mi: And where [we] visited with Akane is?
16 Mo: Kitano Zoo. (1 s).
17 Mi: And where [we] visited long ago, when [I was] a baby?
18 Mo: When [you were] a baby, Umeno Park.
19 Mi: Yeah, right. (1 s) Was Mina cute as a baby?
20 Mo: So cute.

Mina is 4/6 years old. The names of persons and places are pseudonyms. Mi = Mina; Mo = mother; ( ) = short answer and duration of silence (approx. figure); [ ] = contextual and additional information including pronouns omitted in conversation; … = short pause.

In this example, one of the basic characteristics of meaning construction is its development through the flow of interaction. Concretely, the description of Mina in babyhood as a "cute" girl is not achieved as a question and answer pair, as we saw in the beginning, but from a series of interactions that include a variety of topics. A bus on the street leads to the mother's question concerning a bus and their visit to a zoo (line 12),

---

[2] The excerpts included in this chapter are from longitudinal recordings of conversations between a young girl, Mina, and her mother, who lived in a rural area of Japan (about 80 km from the center of Tokyo) (Komatsu, 2006). The recordings were made during their car rides, usually on the way back home from hoikuen, as well as some other instances of recordings occurring on their way to supermarkets or the hospital. Mina's age was between 4 years 4 months and 5 years 8 months when the recordings were made, and total recording time was 34 h over 153 days of observation. Translation from original Japanese into English was made by the author. For further detail of the recordings and translation, see Chap. 3.

after some explanations to correct Mina's understanding of word usage (lines 3–11). From this question, they talk over their visit to some zoos (lines 13–18). Mina's question concerning herself as a baby is an extension of these exchanges. Although it is difficult to describe everything in the recordings of conversation and ordinary conversations often involve fluctuations, we must grasp the interaction with a wider perspective to understand the process and the result of meaning construction.

This example also illustrates that the meaning construction is embedded in the contexts we live in. The starting point of the episode—Mina's witnessing a bus on the street—suggests at least some of our meaning construction comes from accidental encounters when we move around our surroundings. However, determining the specific elements in our environments that enable us to start the interaction is difficult. A bus *can* work as a starting point of a talk about the past, but it does not always inspire the same kind of talk. In other words, it just *happened* to be the cause of interaction in this instance. Thus, what is essential is the composition of our daily lives that enables us to encounter a variety of objects that have a potential to start our meaning construction.

Another aspect of interaction we must consider is that it constructs our relationships for the future. When a child asks her mother if she was cute, what she expects is not a correct and precise description of her babyhood but rather a *feeling* of an intimate and warm relationship with her mother. Although difficult to explain by reference to specific words or utterances in their conversation, this is also an aspect of who Mina was in relation to her mother, and it creates a mood or an atmosphere that canalizes the interaction afterwards. Thus, the self we can observe in meaning construction is not limited to what was described, but also includes what was brought about as the result of relational work.

A Need for a New Perspective for Looking at the Self in Interaction

The characteristics of meaning construction discussed above do not fit with the framework of psychological research that relies on objectivity and reproducibility in its understanding of human mind. The interaction depends on context and starts whimsically, and these characteristics make it hard to replicate. However, considering the irreversible nature of time, all psychological phenomena are essentially one-time events; *we* find (or even construct) the resemblance between two independent events. Thus, what we must pursue for the generalization of findings is not reproducibility but rather the construction of a theoretical framework that fits with the diverse meaning constructions in which we engage in our lives.

In relation to this one-time nature of the episodes of conversation, I must point out that existing psychological inquiries were not concerned with the *reasons* why children talk about their experiences. In many studies that analyzed conversations concerning children's experiences, researchers just asked children and their parents to talk about topics congruent with some academic standards set by the researchers (e.g., Haden, Haine, & Fivush, 1997). This is an attempt to control the settings of interaction to argue for the reproducibility and generalizability of their findings. However, if we attempt to construct a framework that properly explains our meaning construction *embedded in contexts*, observation of what happens in natural settings is an important requirement for investigation. In other words, *we must wait for* the occurrence of meaning construction.

The relational work achieved in the conversations is also difficult to describe or categorize with objective standards. The intimate relationship between a young girl and her mother both mentioning the girl's cuteness is what *we feel* from the series of their meaning construction. However, what we understand from these interactions is not necessarily congruent with children's subjective experiences; *we construct* this relational effect, by becoming a pseudo-participant in the conversation through reading the transcript and employing our imagination. This requires us to focus on *our* work of understanding in inspecting the data, rather than simply considering that what we find is objective and self-evident.

It is also related to a need to have a wider view of interaction to understand the process in which who the child is (or was) becomes clear in meaning construction. What is achieved in an episode of interaction is not reducible to the effect of a specific word or utterance. However, in the analysis, the rambles within an interaction that are the part of whole processes are often considered noise that hides an elementary aspect of how we describe ourselves.

These discussions lead to the consideration that we need a theoretical framework to investigate children's meaning construction and their selves emerging in the process that differs from existing approaches to understanding what children's selves are. In concrete terms, a new perspective must include following orientations:

1. Looking at the process of meaning construction achieved through the continual dynamics that language or *signs* provide, rather than breaking down the interaction into units of words or turns and then aggregating them by several categories.
2. Considering the position of researchers or observers who investigate the process, by imaginarily participating in the interaction and finding what is achieved throughout the process of meaning construction, rather than relying on a concept of objectivity that presupposes what is happening is entirely self-evident to everyone.
3. Approving the one-time-only nature of our meaning construction, including an exploration of their whimsical occurrences, rather than emphasizing the generalization of findings through reproducibility.

In my discussion that follows, I analyze the recordings of mother-child conversations and children's writings about their experiences to understand how we figure out children's selves in meaning construction, based on the perspective I have described above. In the next section, as a starting point for this theoretical inquiry, I introduce an example that typically shows a child's self emerging through meaning construction.

Meaning Construction and an Emergence of the Self in Natural Interaction

When we discuss the self, others often play important roles as, for example, counterparts or opponents to clarify the self in relationships. As I will discuss later in Chaps. 3 and 4, the inquiry here also focuses on how others work in the process through which we find the selves of children. From the corpus of mother-child conversation from which Excerpt 1.1 is derived, here I introduce another episode in which they talk about Mina's experiences at hoikuen. The topic of the excerpt below is about who plays what in their "theater performance" at hoikuen.

Excerpt 1.2
(Komatsu, 2010, p. 215, Excerpt 1, cited with minor modifications, original Japanese in Komatsu (2006))

1 Mo: What is Saito Taku [Mina's friend, boy] (yes) going to play in the theater performance? (1 s).
2 Mi: A bat. (2 s) And Mina [I play] a rabbit.
3 Mo: In the dance by the rabbits? The bat? (1 s) [Does he appear in] Another dance?
4 Mi: After the bats, (uh hum) then maybe rabbits, (hmm) bunny rabbits.
5 Mo: Mimi, the bunny ... Oops [I guess I was] wrong, snow rabbits!
6 Mi: Mina, the snow rabbit xx [inaudible].
7 Mo: Mina is [You are] a moon rabbit, aren't you? (Oh, [you are] right) A yellow rabbit, aren't you?
8 Mi: [I'm] Not a snow rabbit. (1 s) xx [inaudible]?
9 Mo: A flower rabbit. (Wrong) Mina, the moon rabbit.
10 Mi: That's right. Sayuri [Mina's friend, girl] and Sada Miki [Mina's friend, girl] play flower rabbits, don't they? (yes) Iiyama Mina and Sanae [Mina's friend, girl] are, well, moon rabbits, two moon rabbits and (yes) the white rabbit is, well, Tano (1 s) Tanokura (yes) Tano ... Tanokura, yeah, Tanokura Nagisa [Mina's friend, girl].
11 Mo: Tanokura Nagisa.
12 Mi: And then, Matsuzaka Aika [Mina's friend, girl] (yes) Machida Mina, [Mina's friend, girl] (yes) [you] see?
13 Mo: Yes, [I] see.
14 Mi: Three girls do that together, right?
15 Mo: Yes, but Mina [you] play in two, don't you?
16 Mi: Yes, and also Sayuri [plays] in two. (Yes) And Matsuzaka Aika [plays] in th, three. (Yes) (3 s) Three girls do (yes) that together, right? (2 s) Machida Mina (1 s) is ... one [meaning 'first'] ... see? (1 s) And Sayuri is two ['second']. Mina is three ['third']. That's the way [you] memorize, right?
17 Mo: Yes.

Mina is 4/4 years old. See also footnotes of Excerpt 1.1

Although the interaction begins with the mother's question about one of Mina's friends (Saito Taku), the first half of the interaction (lines 1–9) centers on "who Mina was" in relation to the roles she played. After clarifying the relationship between "bats" and "rabbits," they introduce a variety of rabbits appearing in the performance. Mina attempts to attach the roles to herself arbitrarily (line 6), and her mother corrects her (line 7). Following this, the mother introduces another type of rabbit (line 9). Although the role Mina plays is unclear, here Mina and her mother construct a list of roles through this interaction. Based on this list or frame, in the latter half of the interaction (lines 10–18) Mina begins to describe who plays what. In this interaction, "rabbits" reappear with Mina's friends and the child and her mother discuss the arrangements for the performance. This is also a clarification of Mina's position in the group of young girls.

The description above shows that *I* found Mina and her mother constructing and elaborating a *configuration* of children that also clarifies who Mina was, based on the roles they play. Here I use the word "configuration" because the transcript enables us to construct one unified figure that describes both Mina and her friends within relationships. It is not reducible to any of the turns they took in conversation but instead appears from the whole of the episode. In this configuration, Mina is clearly shown as a member of a group of young girls who are similar in their roles but different as people (see Chap. 2 for further discussion).

As I discussed in the previous section, my understanding here is not the same as what the mother and her daughter felt in this conversation, but rather my version of understanding who Mina was. For example, the names of Mina's friends have different effects for meaning construction for me and for them. Because of this, what we find in this example must be described with concepts that reflect the relational nature of interaction and meaning, not the objective abilities or dispositions of the study participants.

What Works for Our Meaning Construction: Focusing on Two Aspects of Interaction

After introducing an example that presents the figure of a child through meaning construction, the next step is an inspection of the foundations at work in our understanding of it. For this understanding, I will point out two types of discursive acts working here to clarify who Mina was in relation to others.

First, Mina locates herself in an array of same-aged peers and the roles they play. In the first half of the conversational episode, Mina and her mother introduce several "rabbits." This was done somewhat vaguely but in the latter half, the set of roles works well for Mina to establish her position in relation to many of her friends who play different roles in the performance. Here, the set of roles and the listing of friends work as an *enumeration*: a discursive act that "*evokes a homogeneous referential ensemble to which the enumerated constituents refer*" (Dubois & Sankoff, 2001, p. 285). For observers, and possibly for Mina and her mother, the descriptions of other "rabbits" clarify the relationship in which Mina becomes positioned. Looking at the episode of their zoo visit in Excerpt 1.1, which was observed about 2 months after Excerpt 1.2, Mina was also trying to enumerate the places she visited, though it is not clear as in Excerpt 1.2.

Second, in accomplishing this discursive act, Mina and her mother are taking their positions in relation to each other. In the first part of the excerpt, the mother asks several questions concerning her daughter's experiences and also corrects her speech. Here, the conversation heavily relies on the mother's scaffolding to maintain the interaction and clarify the topic. In the latter half, Mina takes a position to *teach* her mother about her experiences. Mina sometimes confirms her mother's understanding (see lines 12–17) as teachers do to their pupils, though this is still dependent on her mother's taking the role of pupil. It is not as distinctive or strategic as the original discussion concerning positioning (Harré & van Langenhove 1999) presupposed. However, this is interpretable as an act of positioning in this local context, as "all conversations always involve some sort of positioning" (Harré & van Langenhove 1999, p. 29). This sort of positioning is less clear in Excerpt 1.1. Yet, as I pointed out, Mina's confirming that she was a "cute baby" can be understood as constructing an intimate relationship with her mother. Thus, the child is clarifying herself in relation to her mother, the partner in conversation.

These two aspects of one excerpt interact to clarify the young girl's self, or who Mina was, *in relation to others:* i.e., her friends appearing in the conversation and her mother as a partner in the interaction. This explanation relies on the concepts developed in research on discourse analysis and doesn't guarantee that the description of Mina observed here is particularly important for her, or that it reflects her stable internal figure of herself, if there is such an internal psychological existence. However, it does indicate how they constructed the interaction to present a configuration to us.

In addition, and as the most important aspect of this framework, what is not included in this discussion of positioning and enumeration is *our* active orientation that merges them into one integrated presentation of Mina. Although the discussions in the discourse analysis are conscious about the relationship between the text and its effects, they focus on the relativistic nature of their understanding and their position in political or academic contexts (see Parker, 2015). In other words, they do not focus on the process of how signs work to present what we understand in the episode as a whole. In the next chapter, I approach what occurs in *who reads the text,* considering theories that focused on the function of signs in human perception, and introduce the analyses and discussions I will undertake.

Chapter 2
Self as Gestalt Quality

If we understand our conversation as a flow of interaction or negotiation, the self I attempted to describe in the introducing chapter is not attributable to a specific utterance by the child or her mother. In other words, inspecting and categorizing each turn separately, as in many qualitative or quantitative approaches to psychology, tells us little about the positions of the participants in the configuration or the portrayal of the child in the relationship. We find the act of positioning in the *sequence* of turns and the relationship between them, and the figure of Mina emerges in resemblances and differences among her friends and herself. Thus, the emerging process of the self I discuss here must be understood in light of how we figure out it. Concerning this point, I connect the essential attribute of the self as discussed here and the concept of *Gestalt quality* (as exemplified by von Ehrenfels in 1890; see von Ehrenfels, 1988a) for observers, and attempt to show the validity of this perspective in relation to several classical and important theories concerning the nature of signs and meaning.

Emergence of the Self and Gestalt Quality

A focus on the holistic nature of human recognition existed in the early phase of psychology. In 1929, von Ehrenfels (1988a), a key figure in the development of Gestalt concepts in psychology, proposed the concept of Gestalt qualities. This is what appears in our minds from a configuration of elements that have relationships to each other. He defined Gestalt qualities as follows:

> By a *Gestalt quality* we understand a positive content of presentation bound up in consciousness with the presence of complexes of mutually separable (i.e., independently presentable) elements. That complex of presentations which is necessary for the existence of a given Gestalt quality we call the *foundation* [Grundlage] of that quality. (p. 93)

He used the example of music and notes below to introduce the concept of Gestalt qualities, showing that what we observe in the configuration of elements is

© The Author(s) 2019
K. Komatsu, *Meaning-Making for Living*, SpringerBriefs in Psychology,
https://doi.org/10.1007/978-3-030-19926-5_2

not reducible to single elements. When a German folk tune was played in F sharp major after having been played in C major, the similarity between the melodies was evident, although the two did not have a single note in common. However, if we play the notes that constitute the original melody in a different order, no such similarity appears. Thus, we find a figure, a melody of a tune, arising from the relationships between notes as one type of Gestalt quality.

In the example of notes and tune, the order or sequential connection of each note is important, and in the music we enjoy, notes are strictly categorized according to their dispositions as pitch or length. However, it is not only in the sequential order of such systematized elements that we find the Gestalt quality. Von Ehrenfels (1988b) also argued that multiple aspects of our recognition have a disposition as a Gestalt quality, as follows:

> Every word of a language is a Gestalt quality. One can form some idea of the extent of Gestalt qualities in psychical life from the fact that the so-called laws of association operate much more frequently in relation to Gestalten than in relation to elements. Thus, for instance, with the image of an individual person, which is (certainly physically and in all probability psychically) a Gestalt quality, there are associated numerous images of other persons according to the law of similarity […]. (p. 122)

The examples and definition of von Ehrenfels resonate with what occurs when we find Mina's self in an episode of conversation. Although we do not know any details about the children mentioned in the conversation, we construct an image of a girl who belongs to a group of rabbits, and who reports this to her mother in a somewhat bossy way, which also implies the receptive and warm nature of their relationship. It is not the sum total of divided pieces of interaction but what emerges from the whole of a configuration they construct in this episode. It is difficult to suppose the uniformity of the images each of us has, but we construct images within our meaning construction through the interaction I presented *and* our resources to understand what we see there.

Relying on the term presentation (*Vorstellung* in German) that von Ehrenfels consistently used to describe the process, I coined the term *presentational self*. It comes up as a Gestalt quality through the activity of meaning construction (e.g., mother-child conversation) and active integration of the observer (Komatsu, 2010, p. 220). It is defined as a genre of self that emerges from the act and the result of meaning construction—here, the configuration of a child and others in conversation— "that creates unique meaning to observers" (Komatsu, 2010, p. 209). The presentational self is essentially relational in a variety of aspects and this contrasts with the notion of *representation* prevailing in psychological research, which presupposes that the self exists independently of the observer.

Presentation as a Mode of Symbolism

The standpoint I take here stresses the process in which an episode of conversation works as a whole to generate a presentation in observers' perception, and this may be comparable with the understanding of works of art. For example, although it is possible and often useful to know how a painting was painted and how its composition functions, our experience of viewing a painting is not derived from single details, nor from the sum total of what we think about the divided sections of one painting. This also applies to pieces of music; that is, what we feel from a piece of music is not our understanding of specific techniques used in the composition, nor the aggregate of what we feel from each note or measure, though specialists may sometimes focus on such details.

Further, our understanding constructed from what we have observed can go beyond what is described and clarify something about who made it. For example, what we find in a landscape painting by Vincent van Gogh is not an analog of the real view but the workings of the mind of a painter who depicted his experiences. Just as van Gogh wanted people to understand his unique feel of the world through his paintings, we can understand how children find the meaning of their experiences to construct figures of themselves from what they express as a whole.

In regard to this holistic orientation for the understanding of the self, I can detect several predecessors in the psychological literature before quantification and statistical analysis ruled our approaches to the mind. One of them is the philosopher Susanne Langer, who proposed a new conception of "mentality" focusing on the function of symbols to oppose the "physical world-picture" that was beginning to have a major impact on psychology at the time of her discussion. In her discussion, Langer (1948) focused on the comparison between *discursive* form and *presentational* form of symbolism. About discursive form, she explains as follows:

> [...] all language has a form which requires us to string out our ideas even though their objects rest one within the other; as pieces of clothing that are actually worn one over the other have to be strung side by side on the clothesline. This property of verbal symbolism is known as *discursiveness*; by reason of it, only thoughts which can be arranged in this peculiar order can be spoken at all; any idea which does not lend itself to this "projection" is ineffable, incommunicable by means of words. (pp. 65–66)

Regarding this clarification, and in relation to what is "ineffable" and "incommunicable," she illustrates presentational aspects of our recognition:

> Visual forms—lines, colors, proportions, etc.—are just as capable of *articulation*, i.e., of complex combination, as words. But the laws that govern this sort of articulation are altogether different from the laws of syntax that govern language. The most radical difference is that *visual forms are not discursive*. (p. 75)

After these discussions, Langer (1948) introduced "presentational symbolism" as what "are involved in a simultaneous, integral presentation" (p. 79), which stands together with discursive form. In her discussion, presentational form is not limited to visual expression and has a close relationship with our feelings, and a variety of presentations such as paintings, music, or metaphor that demand a recognition we cannot reduce to articulate reasoning. She stressed the importance of the presentational aspect of symbolism, which had not been the object of philosophical thinking until that time, aiming to introduce an epistemology of medium and meaning (Innis, 2009), and her idea of presentational form has a close relationship with the discussion of Gestalt psychology, as Langer herself repeatedly introduced in her discussion.

Langer (1948) understood that some aspects of our recognition cannot be divided into elements that comply with those approaches to psychology which rely on statistical empiricism. Although this idea supports my approach for the self here, her discussion of two distinctive forms concentrated only on the symbolism. Concerning the *meaning* they construct, she supposed many types of emergence in our minds. She also denied the correspondence between types of meaning and symbolic forms, as "The sense of a word may hover between literal and figurative meaning" (p. 229). Thus, finding out children's selves from conversation, as I attempt here, is the construction of figurative meaning from the symbols of discursive form, and the focus must be on the semiotic process in which meaning emerges from symbols.

The Complexity of Meaning Construction: Vygotsky's Perspective

From Langer's perspective, even one word is capable of bringing us a variety of meaning. She supposed that every word had many associations and significance in history and suggested that "[…] through all the metamorphoses of its meaning, such a word carries a certain trace of every meaning it has ever had, like an overtone, and every association it acquired, like an aura […]" (Langer 1948, p. 229). Here the meaning of a word, or other discursive symbol, broadens in a fluid way according to the contexts in which we mention it.

When we elaborate this process of finding meaning from words or other discursive acts, Vygotsky's discussion on language and meaning functions as a good guide. His discussion concerning the understanding of meaning and language (Vygotsky, 1986) and how fables, stories, dramas, and poems work for our mind (Vygotsky, 1971) focused on our integrative perception of meaning. Vygotsky (1986) stressed the need to discover a unit of analysis that would reflect the unity of affective aspect *and* intellectual aspect of a dynamic meaning system when we study children's language. In relation to the meaning appearing from a set of expressions, he also gave an example in which a very small change in the usage of a word appearing in a poem by Heine can reshape what we understand from the whole of the poem.

These discussions also suggest the complex nature of meaning that cannot be reduced into simple correspondence between what we see as a sign and what we feel and understand from that. Langer's discussion focused on the historical roots of such extension, and Vygotsky (1986) also discussed the development of meaning in history, in relation to children's thinking in complexes. After pointing out this indeterminate nature of word meaning, Vygotsky (1986) proposed the comparison of *sense* and *meaning* to better understand the process of meaning construction as follows:

> The first and basic one is the preponderance of the *sense* [*smysl*] of a word over its *meaning* [*znachenie*] –a distinction we owe to Frederic Paulhan. The sense of a word, according to him, is the sum of all the psychological events aroused in our consciousness by the word. It is a dynamic, fluid, complex whole, which has several zones of unequal stability. Meaning is only one of the zones of sense, the most stable and precise zone. (pp. 244–245)

His discussion also focused on how a story works on our mind, uncovering the fundamental structure in which we, as readers or observers, play an indispensable role. Concerning the understanding of Hamlet, Vygotsky (1971) argued that the ideas of the story are not reducible to the summary of the story, and only direct descriptions of concrete situations can express them. Again, his approach stresses the importance of our viewing the whole of the story, with our identification with the main character and our feeling of the conflicting affective powers making the flow of story. He also pointed out our dual perspectives in this process, one of which identifies with Hamlet and another that views the entire story from outside. Thus, the story first becomes possible through the integrating work of *our* minds.

These discussions suggest that what we feel from a discursive act, as in the mother-child conversation, emerges from the flow of interaction that fixes the relationship of elements—a variety of "rabbits" described, for example. It unfolds for each person who activates and constructs the *meaning* in his or her own sense field. In this process, we must consider the uniqueness of what emerges for a young girl, for her mother, and for us. The *understanding* of an interaction is not the examination of a fixed object but the re-construction of semiotic processes that bring about the meaning of it. But how can we figure out such processes?

A Semiotic Approach for the Site of Meaning Construction

Although the discussion in the former chapter began by citing the ideas in discourse analysis, now the exploration concerning meaning construction leads us to a question concerning the framework for understanding the work of signs in our life. The thinking of semiotic psychology (Valsiner, 2007), which stresses the role of signs to create meanings in the world in which we are constantly moving through, elaborated the function of signs as what "can function as a promoter sign, guiding the possible range of variability of meaning construction in the future" (Valsiner, 2007, p. 58), and it also constructed the basic understandings of this process.

As we have already discussed, the meaning developing from a word has a vast range of possibility, and semiotic psychology considers that signs work within that field, not in fixed or static ways but rather developing with dialectic dynamics they include as their essential nature. They work both intra-personally and inter-personally to, for example, construct the meaning of our experiences, add value to the objects we encounter, or promote our actions. The self, or "who we are," also becomes emergent through the system of signs. In Valsiner's example of a person who says to himself or herself, "I like this," when observing a painting, the statement not only clarifies his or her affect and guides conduct afterwards (e.g., buying a postcard of the picture), but also clarifies his or her unique perspective to the picture. We are constantly in this sort of dialogue, in relation to external others or objects, including socially shared firm beliefs (Valsiner, 2007), and this *clarifies the position of the person that can be considered the self in relationships.*

Thus, the theory of semiotic psychology describes the relational and dynamic aspect of emerging meaning and the self. Methodological inquiry based on the semiotic approach also stresses the importance of understanding the relational nature of and researchers' positions in the process of research. To describe this complex, Valsiner (2017) introduced a figure to position "four infinities" at work in the interaction of interviewing, or in other types of researcher-participant interaction. Among these four types of infinity, "future infinity" and "past infinity" are what develop through the process of interaction. Taking an example from Excerpt 1.1, recollection of zoo visits is an extension from the here-and-now to *past infinities* in meaning construction.

The position of the researchers is also clear in this schema. In relation to the researcher and the participants, it presupposes the "inner infinity" of researchers and "outer infinity" of participants. Concerning this, Valsiner (2017) describes the scientific knowledge developing in such interactions as "both objective and subjective at the same time" and as "knowledge that is felt through by the researcher" (p. 48). In other words, researchers' understanding is not strictly governed by objectivity.

The difference between the framework of Valsiner (2017) and what I discuss here is the construction of a contact point between researcher and participant. As Valsiner presupposed direct contact between researchers and study participants, the data I will show in this monograph are interactions between mother and child, or teacher and children, and we stand outside of the interaction. Reflecting this difference, Fig. 5.2 of Valsiner (2017) is modified as Fig. 2.1 to describe the mother-child conversation. As we saw in two examples in Chap. 1, conversation between a young child and her mother often develops from the mother's questions in relation to the

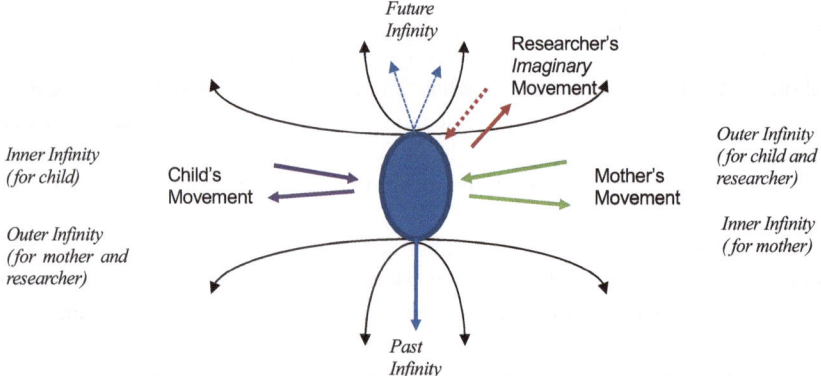

Fig. 2.1 A schematic expression of research field in this study (Cited from Valsiner (2017, p. 48, Figure 5.2), with modifications)

events in their life, while the child also questions what is unclear for her but her mother *knows* (e.g., the name of a zoo they once visited). Although they are not conscious of this structure, it can be interpreted as a variation of reciprocal interviewing in which both participants attempt to construct the meaning of the world that extends from the past to the future, externally and internally. Researchers or observers cannot participate in or control the interaction directly, but can be *quasi-participants* of the interaction, imaginarily sitting in the site of interaction.

Inquiries Into the Self on the Basis of a Semiotic Approach: How Meaning Construction Develops in the Dialectic Tensions in Life

In the following chapters, I will elaborate this theoretical framework that finds children's selves in their meaning construction and stresses the active role of observers, which is essential for understanding the entirety of the process. Relying on the theoretical perspectives discussed above, I will develop a threefold argument.

Firstly, I describe the semiotic process unfolding in conversations in which pairs of young children and their mothers talked about each child's experiences in institutions for young children before school age (yochien and hoikuen), developed from my previous analysis (Komatsu, 2006, 2010, 2013). In contrast with existing studies that sought to find psychological entities inside children as their selves, I elaborate on this process using the framework of dialogical process of meaning construction (Josephs, Valsiner, & Surgan, 1999; Valsiner, 2007), which employs a field-like expression of antithetical concept formation. Using this framework, I argue that the differentiation of shared meaning in conversation enables the appearance of presentational self for observers (Chap. 3). From this elaboration, I attempt to create a fundamental framework of the presentational self and compare it with some psychological inquiries into the self to discuss the generalizability of this concept (Chap. 4).

In the second part of the discussion, I extend my inquiry by analyzing elementary school students' writings about personal experiences (Chap. 5). In Japanese elementary schools, children often engage in writing short personal stories addressed to their teachers and classmates, which report their experiences at home. This activity, with a long historical background in Japanese school education, stands in a contrasting position to the mother-child conversation analyzed in the previous discussion. In the writings, children's meaning construction is achieved through written language, not through oral interaction with clearer dialogical nature. While the mother-child conversation is placed within the children's transition from the institutional setting of formal education to the private and intimate relationship with family members, the writings occupy another area of transition in which the private is brought into formal education. With such contrasts, these activities in the transitions in children's everyday lives also share the characteristic of *liminality* (Turner, 1969) that involves transformation of the processes that sustain our lives (Stenner, 2017). Through the analysis of writings, I also demonstrate the application of the framework of the presentational self and discuss the role of others in the process.

These two analyses lead us to an inquiry into the fundamental processes that bring about the emergence of presentational self. In modern society, children move from a private setting to the institutionalized world every day, and these moves are the moment that triggers the meaning construction. Thus, at least one aspect of children's selves is inseparable with a socially constructed system of transition and reunion. Following from this, the third part of my discussion explores the basic structure of our lives, which sets up a variety of tensions. These structures and tensions interact with each other to build up the background to children's meaning construction. Firstly, I will make an inquiry into our lives focusing on the process of *reunion* that is co-definitive with two types of tension: *visible <> invisible* and *same <> non-same* (Chap. 6). Secondly, I will examine these two dialectic tensions, which are closely related to development in many aspects (Chaps. 7 and 8). Through these inquiries, I focus on the dialectic nature that prevails in our lives, which is also an attempt to answer the question *why* children (and we also) engage in the meaning construction that produces the presentational self.

Chapter 3
Selves Emerging in Meaning Construction: An Analysis of Mother-Child Conversation from a Semiotic Perspective

Every conversation of the child is coloured not only by his individual experience but also by his character, and this must be taken into account if the whole of the meaning is to be extracted from the conversation.

Katz, D. and Katz, R. (1936, p. 11)

From far before the emergence of modern psychology to the present day, oral conversation has been a medium of meaning construction in everyday life. It is not a simple transmission or copying of one's ideas to another person, but rather a collaborative work among participants to develop a shared topic through semiotically mediated processes. Research into conversation analysis and our everyday experiences tells us that, for example, a very short pause or hesitation in the course of conversation sometimes changes the path of meaning construction, and these observations show that natural conversation is very subtle and inconstant work that is difficult to predict

At its beginning, modern psychology attempted to use this flexible and dynamic nature of the dialogical process as one approach to understand the mind. However, with the proliferation of experimental methods stressing reproducibility as a significant advantage and a condition for established science, irregular interactions, especially those in daily life, were omitted from the toolbox of psychology, except for several limited areas of research. From the perspective of studies that attempt to generate some understanding of the mind and clarify the causes of behaviors with experimental methods, everyday interaction appears a mixture of the routine and the whimsical. In other words, we are not conscious of specific *motivations* to undertake routine conduct and this conduct is full of subtle variations. For instance, if a child and her mother have a routine to talk during their car ride, this is not a fixed rule and the topic of discussion changes depending on their mood, or coincidental encounters. However, it is in these whimsicalities that cultural resources work to form our psychological realities. Given this characteristic, daily conversation serves as a beneficial site to inquire into the semiotic processes that lead to the emergence of the

© The Author(s) 2019
K. Komatsu, *Meaning-Making for Living*, SpringerBriefs in Psychology,
https://doi.org/10.1007/978-3-030-19926-5_3

presentational self. In this chapter, starting from this foundational understanding, I explore examples of conversations by pairs of young children and their mothers.

Perspectives on Child Development in Talk

In the history of psychology, natural conversation between children and their parents has already been the subject of investigation to understand child development. As early as 1928, Katz and Katz collected and analyzed over 140 episodes of their sons' conversations (3 years old and 4 years old at the first recording of conversation) over a 1 year period. Their analysis was to aid their understanding of children's development as it appears in their dialogue, and the content of the conversation was considered to show "thinking, feeling and volitional attitudes taken up by the child towards his environment in general" (Katz and Katz, 1936, p. 5). They also attempted to understand the "character" of their two sons from the conversation and their observations.

Although their analysis was a simple series of interpretations concerning the episodes they observed, they clearly understood the utility of natural conversation to understand the children's minds. In their analysis, they stressed the importance of analyzing the conversational interaction as a whole, not dividing it into pieces, insisting that the conversation was "experienced by the participants themselves as a unity (p. 25)." They also pointed out the dialogical nature of conversation and the inadequacy of reporting one fragment of a child's utterance without clarifying the context.

Despite this pioneering study, researchers of developmental psychology did not consider the analysis of natural conversation as a major method. This aversion may stem, at least partially, from the lack of reproducibility of natural conversation in comparison with experimental methods or structured interviews. Subsequently, it was the sociolinguistic and anthropological approaches for child development that discovered the importance of analyzing verbal interactions in natural settings. With a focus on the process of linguistic socialization, Heath (1983) collected ethnographic data in two rural communities in the United States and described the differences in linguistic environments for children, in relationship with school education. Heath (1983) made detailed descriptions of "oral traditions" of these communities, which included ways of telling personal stories to others, as one concern within linguistic socialization studies is how personal storytelling is practiced. Thus, many studies discussed ways of personal storytelling, focusing on tellability—i.e., what is worth talking about (Aukrust, 2002)—or the structure of participation (e.g., who has the right to tell a story) (Blum-Kulka, 1997), with analysis of makeup of the stories.

Given this attention to the storytelling in natural conversation, researchers discussed its importance in a variety of ways, and did not concentrate on how children learn culturally specific ways of telling. For example, they pointed out its importance in children's understanding of the *reason* for people's behaviors or how events occur (Blum-Kulka, 2002), and cultural norms (Georgakopoulou, 2002; Pontecorvo, Fasulo, & Sterponi, 2001). Studies of conversation analysis also supposed that sharing stories in daily conversation is important for maintaining our interpersonal relationships. That is, when participants engage in collaborative narration of a family story, it works "to ratify group membership and modulate rapport" (Norrick, 2000, p. 154). Middleton and Brown (2005) discussed the co-remembering by a young child and his mother as a construction of family membership. As Bamberg (2011) pointed out, what works in these instances is not *big* (biographical) stories but *small* stories. If the whole of a story is not shared, only repeating other speakers' words, phrases, or sentences "serves an over-arching purpose of creating interpersonal involvement" (Tannen, 1989, p. 52). These studies suggested that conversation concerning children's experiences works as a site of children's linguistic, cognitive, and social development.

Personal Storytelling and the Development of Children's Selves

In relation to a variety of interests pursued in linguistic socialization studies, Miller et al. (1990) pointed out that several types of interaction observed in ethnographical research are interpretable as the construction of children's selves: that is, "coming to express and understand who one is" (p. 305), citing the theoretical framework of social constructionism and Vygotsky's ideas. Miller et al. (1990) hypothetically proposed three types of storytelling—adults telling stories about children; adults and older children intervening in children's storytelling; and children appropriating others' stories—that are closely related to the construction of children's selves. Miller et al. (1992) further developed this concern by focusing on interpersonal relationships appearing in children's personal stories, and attempted to understand children's selves *in relation to others.*

The discussions by Miller and her colleagues indicated the role of others, both as partners in conversation and as the ones appearing in the stories, to clarify the self of children in their storytelling. From this fundamental interest, they made several cross-cultural comparisons of ethnographical data and discussed the differences in the ways children's past conduct was narrated. Among all this research, Wiley, Rose, Burger, and Miller (1998) presupposed that "children come to enact certain kinds of selves by virtue of their everyday participation with other people in characteristic self-relevant practices" (p. 833), and called this practice *selfways,* citing Markus, Mullally, and Kitayama (1997). This perspective on children's selves emphasizes how children's participation in personal storytelling is managed and performed to clarify the autonomous selves of the children, and shows the possibility of finding out children's selves in the ways storytelling is performed. Among the studies of conversation analysis, there also is an attempt to describe children's selves in the relationships *described in the stories.* Levine's (2007) study analyzed the talk between a 4 year-old child and his parents and discussed the significance of talking about the neighborhood to situate themselves within a physical and social *landscape*. Thus, talking about a child's surroundings helps carve out who he or she is in his or her environment.

These studies show that two aspects of conversation discussed in the previous chapters—that is, relationships described through conversation and the relationship participants of the conversation construct—have already been adopted in several studies and have showed their potential. However, existing studies also suggest that there is room for discussing and elaborating theoretical frameworks that enable an integrative account concerning the self that emerges in these two aspects of the conversational interaction, rather than reducing it to a mere "cultural difference."

Focus on the Conversation Concerning Everyday Transition in Children's Lives

To inquire into the self emerging through conversation, I analyzed recordings of mother-child conversations concerning children's experiences in institutions for young children (yochien and hoikuen; see footnote 1 of Chap. 1) (Komatsu, 2006, 2010, 2013). Although several studies of linguistic socialization (Aukrust, 2002) and early childhood education (Bradbard, Endsley, & Mize, 1992) discussed this topic of conversation, they did not fully identify its uniqueness and possible advantages. In concrete terms, Aukrust (2002) focused on the tellability of several topics but did not discuss the meaning of these topics in relation to child development. Bradbard et al. (1992) only showed parental responses to several items in a questionnaire. For this reason, I will show several reasons why I examine this conversation before analyzing the recordings in detail, citing the results of preliminary inquiries using a questionnaire for mothers.

Firstly, at least in Japan, this genre of conversation is frequent among young children and their mothers, and often includes some discussion of the children's interpersonal relationships. In responses from 581 mothers to a questionnaire asking about the frequency and content of their conversations about their children's experiences at yochien, nearly 90% of the mothers indicated that this topic came up every day, and around half of the mothers answered that they discussed this topic for more than 10 min on average (Komatsu, 2000, 2013). The mothers' answers also showed that frequent topics of conversation include children's interpersonal experiences in yochien: for example, nice things that teachers or friends did for children, or troubles or quarrels among similarly aged children (Komatsu, 2003). Although these answers rely on the mothers' subjective reports, it is plausible that these topics would appear on a daily basis, and these are often relatively long exchanges among family members with young children.

Secondly, in relation to the prevalence of this topic, these conversations are at work in the transition between two qualitatively different interpersonal relationships: namely, children's relationships among their same-aged peers, and their close relationships with family members. As already mentioned in Chap. 1, this transition places the child's relational position in an area of liminality (Turner, 1969), where one's identity becomes uncertain. This liminal nature also works for mothers who take part in these conversations. The mothers' answers to the questionnaire show that mothers usually attach great importance to these conversations, especially in order to understand and share their children's experiences (Komatsu, 2000, 2013). The prevalence of these conversations is related to the mothers' positive attitude to them, and thus these conversations are uniquely positioned in the daily lives of young children.

The characteristics of these conversations offer favorable conditions for inquiring into how children's selves are clarified through interpersonal relationships. Although my discussion draws from a limited number of mother-child pairs, the mothers' answers to the questionnaire suggest that the interactions appearing in the excerpts are not limited to these pairs but are applicable to other families in Japan.

Data Collection and Preliminary Analysis

In the following discussion, I use data from longitudinal recordings of conversations by two pairs of mothers and their children who attended hoikuen or yochien. The recordings were made in the naturalistic settings of each family's ordinary life. Names of all study participants are pseudonyms.

Mina and her mother (Komatsu 2006, 2010) A young girl, Mina, and her mother live in a rural area of Japan (about 80 km from the center of Tokyo) with Mina's father and two older brothers. Longitudinal recordings on the car ride home from hoikuen were employed, following a previous study collecting naturally occurring conversational narratives (Preece, 1987). The mother was informed about the purpose of the recording and consent was obtained. To record conversation in a natural setting, the author emphasized that there was no obligation to talk about the child's experiences. The mother also understood that she could stop the recording at any time and could decline to hand over the recordings to the author if she or another family member did not want another person to hear them.

The recordings were made during their car rides, mainly on the way back from hoikuen. The majority of other instances of recordings occurred on their way to the supermarket or to the hospital that Mina visited for regular physical examinations, usually after Mina had attended hoikuen. Except for two recordings in which Mina's older brothers were also present, recordings were made when only Mina and her mother were in the car. The recordings were not made in any predetermined or scheduled fashion and there were several gaps in data collection, due to the mother's work schedule and other reasons.

Mina's age was between 4 years 4 months and 5 years 8 months when these recordings were made. The total time of these recordings was 34 h from 153 days of observation, not including preliminary recordings made before this period, which were undated. During the period in which the recordings were made, the author conducted several interviews with the mother to clarify the content of the conversation by obtaining supplemental information about the people or events appearing in the conversation.

Yuuma and his mother (Komatsu 2013) Yuuma (nicknamed Yucchi) is a boy who lives in a city in the greater Osaka area of Japan with his parents and older brothers. Longitudinal recordings of his conversations with his mother were made in their house, mainly after he had returned from a yochien located within walking distance of their house. Before commencing the recordings, the author asked the mother to record only when they were relaxed and had ample time to talk, and she understood that she was in control of when to record and what to give the author, just as with the recordings of Mina's conversation. The recorded conversations were used for this study with the mother's consent.

The recording period was from May of Yuuma's first year in yochien (his age was 5 years 0 months) to March of the second year. (6 years 10 months).[1] Due to the fundamental nature of the recordings, as described in the case of Mina, the frequency, place, and total time of recording per day were not strictly controlled. Total recording time was 59 h from 193 days of observation. Supplemental information concerning the content of the conversation was obtained through interviews with the mother.

Transcription and extraction of episodes From the recordings, detailed transcripts with information about pauses and overlaps were made. In Yuuma's case, detailed transcription was limited to the sections of the recording where they talked about his experiences at yochien. Given the basic intention of the study to examine the interpersonal aspects of children's experiences appearing in conversation, episodes in which Mina or Yuuma and their friends appeared were extracted and used for further examination, though the standards used for extracting these episodes were slightly different between the two pairs. The number of episodes was 50 for Mina and her mother, and 89 for Yuuma and his mother. Details of episodes in relation to the periods of recordings can be found in Komatsu (2010) (Mina corpus) and Komatsu (2013) (Yuuma corpus).

Why Others? The Starting Point of Meaning Construction

In introducing the framework of the presentational self in Chap. 1, I focused on the enumeration of others (Mina's friends) as what constructs the Gestalt quality. Although talking about interpersonal relationships is considered important in the construction of the self, and is already analyzed in Miller et al. (1992), their study focused only on the categorization of the relationships mentioned in storytelling and

---

[1] In Japan, the academic year generally begins in April and ends in March.

did not elaborate the process by which the self becomes clear in the configuration of children. Thus, as a foundation for the analysis of meaning construction processes, here I show how others mentioned in the episodes of conversation function in the process of meaning construction.

First, other people whom children meet outside the home offer unique opportunities for children to figure out who they are. As already pointed out, a child encounters many children of similar age every day in institutions for young children. In theoretical frameworks concerning the development of self-representation (Harter, 1999), children at this age (very early childhood, early to middle childhood) do not rely on the comparison between self and others in their understanding of self: adults are the important others in appreciating children's conduct. However, even though children do not, or cannot, adopt the perspective to evaluate themselves or others through comparison, children are able to observe the same individuals and themselves every day. They are always on the move, providing opportunities for interaction, and there are various affective experiences available. Our "psychological life in its sign-mediated forms is affective in its nature" (Valsiner, 2007, p. 301), and meeting others is one of several crucial events that can lead to such affective experiences.

These interpersonal relationships of children also activate the concern of the parents—the second reason I focus on others in the process of meaning construction. Although children themselves may not consider the importance of interpersonal relationships, parents who talk with their children have a strong interest in the relationships their children make. Maintaining harmonious relationships with friends is an important concern for parents, and conversation serves as a site for understanding these relationships (Komatsu, 2013). As the conversations we analyze are collaborative work between children and parents, in which their concerns become clear, conversations about others hold the potential for rich meaning construction.

In addition to these two reasons, I will point out that both the act and the result of mentioning others have the capability to be a fundamental aspect of clarifying the self. In Excerpt 1.2, roles in the theater performance ("rabbits") worked to identify and clarify the differences between the child talking in the conversation and the others through enumeration. Even without such an explicit framework for enumeration, differentiation between self and others occurs to clarify the child's presentational self. This is because the mere appearance of others, even just as names, reveals the essential commonalities with and differences with the child who is telling her mother stories. Here is an example of some very simple enumeration of self and others as constructed by Mina and her mother.

Excerpt 3.1
(Komatsu, 2010, p. 224, Excerpt 3, cited with minor modifications) [After Mina and her mother have talked about their meeting with the author.]

1 Mo: A man who came that time is Komatsu. That teacher was Mr. Komatsu. (1 s).
2 Mi: Oh. That teacher was Mr. Komatsu! (Yes) (1 s) Well, [his] name sounds like a woman's, doesn't it?

3 Mo: Hmm … but there are many surnames. Family names. Mina's is Iiyama. (1 s) [speaking simultaneously with line 4] Iiya.

4 Mi: Iiyama (yes) Mina, [surname comes first in Japanese] Machida Mina, (yes) ah, Yamashita Sayuri, (yes) Matsuzaka Aika, (yes) Kinoshita Taku, (yes) Honjo Yuto, Toyama Yuuki, Sada Miki, (yes) you know?

5 Mo: Yes.

6 Mi: So many names, aren't there? (Yes) But Mina and Mina are the same. (Yes) Like Machida Mina, Toyama Mina, and Iiyama Mina.

7 Mo: Yes.

Mina is 4/11 years old. The excerpt includes 3 turns immediately before the episode picked up according to the criterion for analysis. Names are pseudonyms except for the author. See footnotes to Excerpt 1.1.

In this episode of conversation, Mina enumerates her friends' names (line 4) after her mother's comment about the variation in surnames. Subsequently, she mentions two of her friends who share the same first name, Mina (line 6). This meaning construction results in an ensemble of children who attend the same hoikuen and sheds light on Mina as one of them. Three young girls share the same first name, but they are different from each other. In addition to this configuration observers construct in their understanding, it is plausible that Mina and her mother had a detailed figure of each child and formed an elaborated Gestalt quality.

This example shows that the inclusion of others in such a collaborative meaning construction is often very effective because it can lead both participants' and observer's search for the relationships among them to construct a unified figure based on the commonalities and differences. In this process, the amount of information about the self and others is not necessarily related to the clarity of the self that the observer discovers. A short but sensible composition of a child and others can bring about the uniqueness of him or her in relationships and of his or her perspective that emerges within the meaning construction.

In addition, the making of a simple list is not separate from the relationship constructed by the participants in the conversation. Again, in this interaction Mina is leading the enumeration and her mother is in the position of follower, though she gives additional information (line 3). Because making a list in conversation has several interpersonal effects, including enhancing rapport between the participants (Tannen, 1989), an interaction as in Excerpt 3.1 also functions in the construction of the relationship between a young child and her mother.

Making Multiple Contrasts of Self and Others: The Role of Culturally Constructed Categories

The configuration of self and others discussed above can develop by integrating many concepts or standards that children contact in their daily lives. Children's experiences in institutional settings like hoikuen are not limited to just encountering a variety of other people, but are broad enough to offer multiple perspectives for looking at others. The theater performance roles appearing in Excerpt 1.2 provide a good example. Each child has a role as an animal, such as "rabbit," that is familiar for children, and the commonalities and differences of these roles create an image in addition to the unique image of each child.

Although categories such as roles in a performance are common in collective activities for young children in Japan, children also introduce different genres of information into conversation to describe their own uniqueness. Toward the end of the Mina corpus, there is an episode of conversation in which a variety of perspectives are integrated in the configuration. Excerpt 3.2 is an extract from this long interaction.

Excerpt 3.2
(Komatsu, 2010, pp. 217–218, Excerpt 2, cited with minor modifications, original Japanese in Komatsu (2006))

1 Mi: Well, like mom, (yes) and [our] teacher decided to play 'mother' [in pretend play]. Nakayama Makoto [Mina's friend, boy] played the child (yes) for Mina's group. (Yes) [It's] Fourth (yes) and then, umm, Makoto (yes) was the child.
[Several turns omitted].

2 Mi: And (yes) older sister was Mina and then, umm, Taka-morita Yuko [Mina's friend, girl].

3 Mo: Taka-morita Yuko, what a long name! (1 s).

4 Mi: [Didn't you] know [her] surname? Mom (don't know) [You] didn't know [her] surname [speaking simultaneously with line 5] Taka-morita.

5 Mo: Ah Yuko! That Yuko is she?

6 Mi: Yes, always [speaking simultaneously with line 7] slow [in eating lunch and doing work].

7 Mo: Always slow Yuko [laughs] ... [I wonder] Who is slower, well, Mina [or Yuko]. Ah, so Taka-morita (yes) is [her] surname (1 s). [She played] An older sister, and?

8 Mi: Yuko can't read Ja Jab Japanese.

9 Mo: Ah, Yuko can't speak Japanese?

10 Mi: Yes, only a little.

11 Mo: Only a little, but [she] can play with everyone very well, can't [she]? Is it ok to play [even if you] can't speak?

12 Mi: Yes, sure. Today, [we] played in a big maze. (Umm) Mee-zu, Mee [Mo laughs] (Yes) And then, the father was (yeah) Nakayama Takashi [Mina's friend, boy] and the mother was a girl with 'O' O O ya ma (yes) and a girl with 'Ri' (Rie!) Ding dong! (2 s). [Her surname] Oyama ... And Rie has a child, (1 s) her younger sister. (Hum) Shall I tell you, mom? (Yes) Ooyama (yes) Chika.

13 Mo: What? [Is she] a real younger sister [of Rie]? Not in the pretend play (yes). (1 s).

14 Mi: And it has nothing to do [with this talk].
15 Mo: [Speaking simultaneously with line 16] Yes.
16 Mi: There, (yes) Rie, (yes) and Makoto, (yes) and you know, Nakayama Taka,
        and Mina, Mina, and Taka-morita Yuko (yes). So only, only,
17 Mo: Only they can play [in Mina's group].
18 Mi: Yes.

Mina is 5/8 years old.

This episode shows a structure in common with Excerpt 1.2: that is, Mina enu-merates her friends on the basis of their roles in a pretend play, and others appearing in this episode construct the grid in which to place Mina, as discussed in the former section. However, there are also several differences in meaning construction in com-parison with Excerpt 1.2. The first is in the configuration of Mina and her friends. In Excerpt 3.2, they are not simply enumerated but described with a variety of charac-teristics (lines 6, 8, and 12) that are observable in hoikuen. These descriptions of her friends are different from the ones in Excerpt 1.2 because they are not from one episode (e.g., a pretend play) but based on Mina's observations or experiences that identify their characteristics. These descriptions of Mina's friends were not evident when Excerpts 1.2 and 3.1 were recorded. Komatsu (2006) shows that Mina's inserting such one-time episodes concerning her friends in instances of conversation began to appear in the corpus a half-year before the episode in Excerpt 3.2 was observed.

By integrating this type of description into the enumeration of friends, the con-figuration of self and others becomes more elaborated, and Mina's multiple view points for arranging her friends and herself become clearer. In this collaborative meaning construction, Mina also acts more skillfully in her positioning in relation to her mother, as she is the one who knows the children and events at hoikuen. For example, she actively presents questions for her mother to guess (lines 4 and 12). Conversely, corrections by the mother of her daughter's misunderstandings as observed in Excerpts 1.2 and 3.1 are not evident. Thus, Mina's self in relation to other(s) is clearer in Excerpt 3.2—not only in her descriptions of others but in the interactive positioning with her mother.

Construction of the Presentational Self as a Development at the Microgenetic Level

The differences between Excerpts 1.2 and 3.2 discussed here are obtained by look-ing at two processes from a single perspective. In Excerpt 3.2, by managing her position more skillfully, Mina is able to add further detail about how she sees her friends and her detailed descriptions of her friends and her experiences also work to position her as an expert on events at hoikuen. Thus, Mina and her mother are now more refined in their use of discursive devices in creating the layout that positions Mina. The interval of 15 months between the two episodes suggests that this difference reflects Mina's linguistic and psychological development.

However, there is no other episode in the recordings that is equally detailed in the description of the self and others as Excerpt 3.2, which indicates that this type of interaction cannot be explained by psychological abilities of the child that enable the repeated emergence of the same type of interaction. Although it is plausible that Mina's vocabulary increased and her cognitive and social understanding was elaborated during this 1 year period, the interactive act of inserting related information concerning her friends cannot be explained by one specific ability that is measurable by a standardized measurement. The relationship-making in the conversation may also be related to the socioemotional characteristics of Mina and her mother. However, the genre of conversation I discussed occurs rarely and it is difficult to know what aspect might reflect this emotional disposition of the pair, even if it is an important prerequisite for a smooth conversation.

Using the framework by Valsiner (2007) that considers human development at three levels, the foregoing discussion suggests that a perspective that finds out the self as a Gestalt quality does not fit with the development at the *ontogenetic* level, especially when it presupposes well-maintained "stable meaning structures that guide the person within one's life course" (Valsiner, 2007, p. 302). The emergence of the self discussed here is the development at the *microgenetic* level that occurs "as the person faces the ever-new next time moment in the infinite sequence of irreversible time" (p. 301). What we can observe here is the result of the meaning construction that is *not* abandoned in the overabundance of semiotic activity. Further, the conversation is also embedded in the context between home and institution, and is mildly guided by "*mesogenetic* constraints" (p. 302; e.g. routine activities): in this case, regular conversations during car rides.

In Valsiner's (2007) framework of semiotic approach, what is happening at each of these three levels (microgenetic, mesogenetic, and ontogenetic) does not demonstrate one-to-one correspondence, and there is no simple relationship between microgenesis and ontogenesis, as in "the frequency of microgenetically similar recurrent events accumulates over time linearly to impact ontogenesis" (p. 303). Thus, it is difficult to know the development at ontogenetic level from the data discussed here. Valsiner also discusses the importance of focusing on the "processes that proceed *between* the different levels": that is, the "affective creation of signs" (p. 305). Following this perspective, I attempt to describe the process by which signs emerge and are used in meaning construction.[2]

---

[2] For a discussion concerning mesogenetic structures, see Chap. 6.

How Signs Work in Conversation: A Description
of the Dialectic Tension of Meaning

How does meaning develop in the conversation and present a complex composition of self and others? As Rommetveit (1992) explained, conversation is the participants' establishing "shared social reality" (p. 23) by reciprocal adjustment of their perspectives. They are "epistemically dependent upon each other and co-responsible for the product" (Rommetveit, 1992, p. 33), and achieve the collaborative sharing of the event by their continual introduction of new perspectives or new information. In this process, "the speaker has the privilege to determine what is being referred to and/or meant, whereas the listener is committed to make sense of what is said, temporarily adopting the speaker's perspective" (Rommetveit, 1985, p. 190). Accordingly, what is shared in one given moment of interaction is not independent from what is shared before that moment. In other words, meaning always has some relationship with what was already shared in the relationship.

In the description of such a process, I adopt a perspective that views the meaning as the oppositions, from the Austrian tradition of psychology with its origin in the work of Franz Brentano, elaborated to *the field of meaning* by Alexius Meinong "who established the foundations of *Gestalt* thought in Graz (Austria) in the 1880s" (Valsiner, 2007, p.158). Meinong (1983) emphasized the dialectic nature of meaning that enables further development. In his framework, apprehension of "**A**" comes with the apprehension of "**non-A**" and these two are asymmetric; that is, **non-A** operates as *negativum* of **A** (Valsiner, 2007). According to Meinong (1983), **non-A** works in our recognition of X that is *not* similar to **A**. Thus, our sharing something (**A**) in conversation is always accompanied by **non-A**, although it is not something explicit and fixed.

From this basic idea, Josephs, Valsiner, and Surgan (1999) developed a theoretical framework of *meanacting* (acting toward creating meaning) in the dialogical processes that sees the sign as what "orients the sign constructer (user) toward the immediately potential future (p. 258)" and introduced the field-like expression of meaning construction (See Fig. 3.1 for example). It shows a complex of united opposites of **A** (e.g., "I played a rabbit today.") and **non-A** that is a semi-open indeterminate field for possible new meanings. For example, the new meaning, "I don't like playing a rabbit" might appear in this field. Although **non-A** is open to new meaning, it exists in relative opposition to **A** and these two are embedded in a completely open context for the sign, **Not-A**. In this relationship, the dialectic tension of **A** <> **non-A** provides the dynamics for new meaning related to the existing meaning.

This schema shows the fundamental structure of meaning construction and does not fit with the orientation for objective categorization of turns in interaction employed by most psychological research. In other words, it is impossible to set an objective standard to find "**A**" in a given interaction, and the framework gives us only a perspective to look at the conversation considering the existence of a dialectic tension that leads to further microgenesis of meaning.

How Meaning Develops in Conversation: Sequence of Differentiation

In natural conversation, the differentiation of meaning occurs in turn-taking. In the excerpt below (from Excerpt 1.2), once Mina has introduced "(bunny) rabbits" in lines 2 and 4 replying to her mother's question, her mother introduces a narrower category of rabbits ("snow rabbits") to the shared area of meaning (line 5). This is a transformation of the shared meaning: that is, an example of differentiation. Following her daughter's identification with "snow rabbits," the mother makes a correction (another differentiation; line 7).

(From Excerpt 1.2)

1 Mo: What is Saito Taku [Mina's friend, boy] (yes) going to play in the theater performance? (1 s).

2 Mi: A bat. (2 s) And Mina [I play] a rabbit.

3 Mo: In the dance by the rabbits? The bat? (1 s) [Does he appear in] Another dance?

4 Mi: After the bats, (uh hum) then maybe rabbits, (hmm) bunny rabbits.

5 Mo: Mimi, the bunny … Oops [I guess I was] wrong, snow rabbits!

6 Mi: Mina, the snow rabbit xx [inaudible].

7 Mo: Mina is [You are] a moon rabbit, aren't you? (Oh, [you are] right) A yellow rabbit, aren't you?

8 Mi: [I'm] Not a snow rabbit. (1 s) xx [inaudible]?

From the perspective of meanacting, this process achieves a *growth of meaning* (Josephs, Valsiner, and Surgan 1999, p. 266). Using the field-like expression by Josephs et al., this interaction is hypothetically described as in Fig. 3.1. In this interaction, I set Mina's introduction of "bunny rabbit" as a point in which a complex of meaning begins to move (**A**), and this provides a latent field for further meaning (**non-A**). **Non-A** exists in relation to **A** (rabbit) but is a potential field of new meaning (e.g., "I play a *doggie* after that"). In the tension between these two fields, the first differentiation in this process happens in field **A**; that is, it is differentiated into the field of **a'**, "a snow rabbit", with **non-a'**. In this field, the mother constructs a new meaning field (designated **a"**), "a moon rabbit," in the **non-a'** area, and Mina follows it (lines 7–8).

In this example, as soon as they share what one utterance means, Mina and her mother differentiate it further. In other words, their sharing of something sets up a proximal zone of differentiation in the interaction. Such smoothness is not always observed, or rather is rare, in the recordings. This is because the microgenesis of meaning is over-abundant and "most of the semiotic devices created are abandoned, some even before their use" (Valsiner, 2007, p. 301). Thus, the meaning construction here somehow *survived* to become explicit. This instability of meaning construction can be explained by multiple dialectic tensions that are closely related to the makeup of this genre of conversation. At the micro level, it is the tension of **A <> non-A** discussed above.[3]

---

[3] Other types of tension are discussed in Chaps. 6–8.

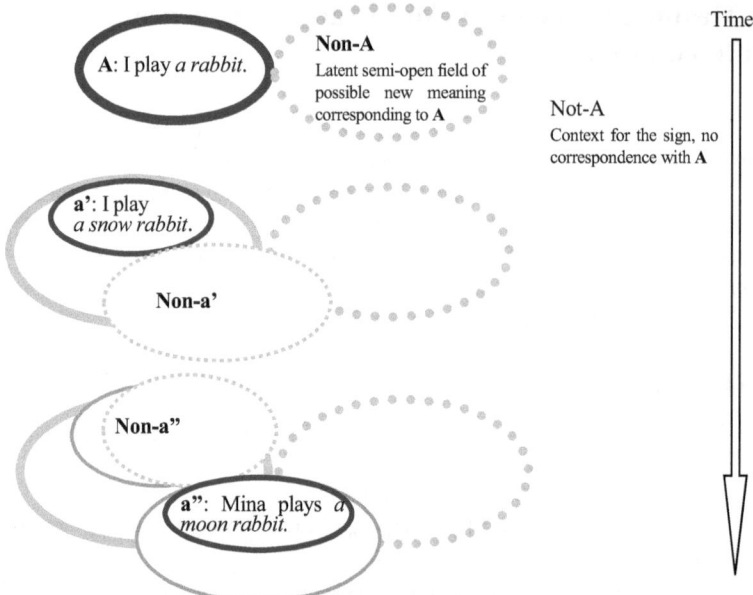

Fig. 3.1 Meaning complexes constituted in the interaction between Mina and her mother (Komatsu, 2010, p. 222, Figure 1, cited with minor modifications)

The positioning of Mina and her mother becomes possible through this sequence of sharing and differentiation, and the process also clarifies both participants' perspectives in relation to each other. In the interaction described above, the mother leads the differentiation, whereas Mina's perspective is not as clear. However, once the complex of meaning—that is, a grid constructed from the roles—appears, Mina begins to use it by clarifying the relationships between the roles and the names of her friends, and assumes a position of teaching these to her mother.

(From Excerpt 1.2)

 9 Mo: A flower rabbit. (Wrong) Mina, the moon rabbit.
10 Mi: That's right. Sayuri [Mina's friend, girl] and Sada Miki [Mina's friend, girl] play flower rabbits, don't they? (yes) Iiyama Mina and Sanae [Mina's friend, girl] are, well, moon rabbits, two moon rabbits and (yes) the white rabbit is, well, Tano (1 s) Tanokura (yes) Tano … Tanokura, yeah, Tanokura Nagisa [Mina's friend, girl].
11 Mo: Tanokura Nagisa.
12 Mi: And then, Matsuzaka Aika [Mina's friend, girl] (yes) Machida Mina, [Mina's friend, girl] (yes) [you] see?

13 Mo: Yes, [I] see.
14 Mi: Three girls do that together, right?
15 Mo: Yes, but Mina [you] play in two, don't you?
16 Mi: Yes, and also Sayuri [plays] in two. (Yes) And Matsuzaka Aika [plays] in th, three. (Yes) (3 s) Three girls do (yes) that together, right? (2 s) Machida Mina (1 s) is ... one [meaning 'first'] ... see? (1 s) And Sayuri is two ['second']. Mina is three ['third']. That's the way [you] memorize, right?
17 Mo: Yes.

Although "white rabbit" (another role? Or another name for snow rabbits?) is newly introduced here, what works in this section of interaction is a configuration of proper nouns: that is, names of Mina's friends. Proper nouns and common nouns are different in their intension, but the name of each friend carries a potential for new meaning related to him or her. In this particular interaction, this potential does not work well and the configuration of children is elaborated only by *tracing* developments in the former interaction—that is, these names are simply imposed upon the grid of roles. In contrast to this relatively simple extension of meaning, Mina uses the grid of related roles to assume a position in relation to her mother. The details of the casting represent information that Mina knows better than her mother, and these details offer her an opportunity to assume the position to *teach* it.

The Potential of Proper Nouns

The interaction in Excerpt 3.2, in which Mina actively introduces her perspective on her friends, shows another example of differentiation in a shared field of meaning. Mina brings up her friend's names in reference to the roles they played (lines 1–2), and this resembles the process in the latter half of Excerpt 1.2 shown above. However, one of her friends, Yuko, serves as a point to extend the field of meaning. Mina's mother first comments the length of her surname, and then Mina mentions some of her personal characteristics. Subsequently, in relation to one of Yuko's characteristics, Mina tells a story about what she did with Yuko that day. These meaning constructions all develop in relation to the young girl Yuko, but they also construct the description of Mina (Fig. 3.2).

This meaning construction is all related to Yuko: that is, the meaning complex described here is within the field of "who Yuko is." Although it is difficult to describe all the processes as a simple plane figure as here, we can see a variety of characteristics appear one after another in relation to her: that is, they are successively *taken over* by new signs (Josephs, Valsiner, and Surgan 1999). These include length of surname (lines 3–4), slowness of eating lunch (lines 5–7), linguistic ability (lines 8–11), and an episode of play (lines 11–12). In relation to this meaning construction concerning Yuko, who Mina is in relation to her also becomes clear. She is a rival in

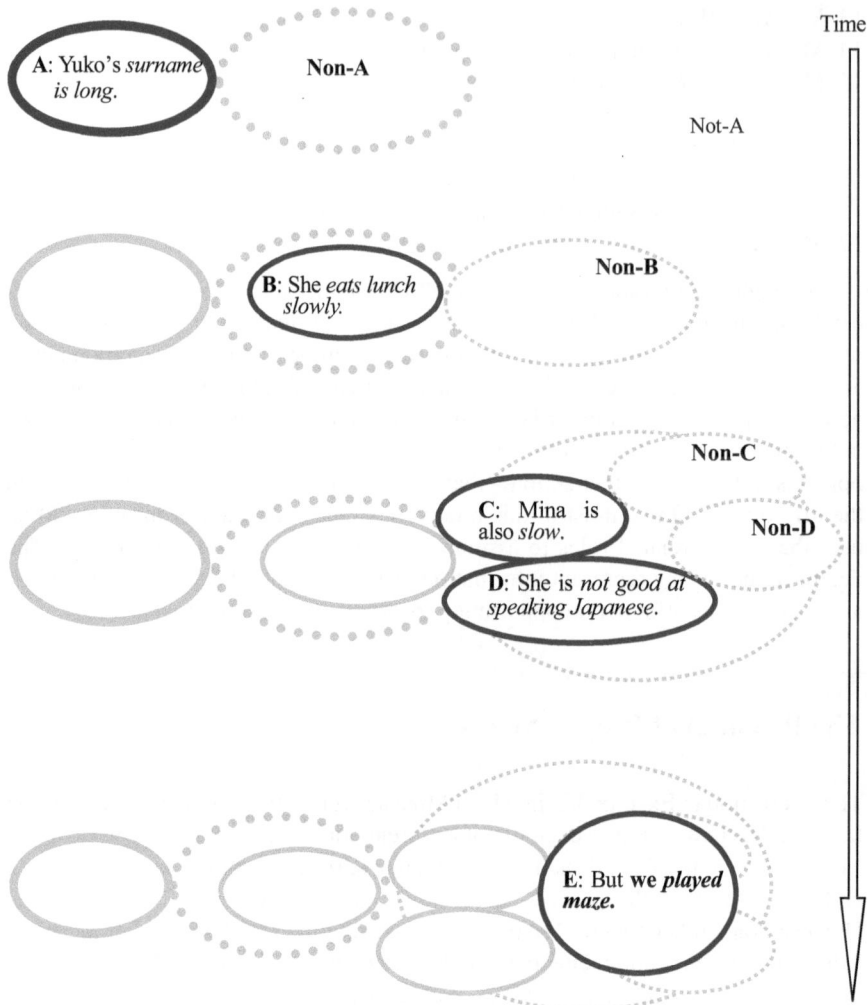

Fig. 3.2 Meaning complexes constituted concerning Yuko and Mina

slowness of eating lunch (although this is only indicated by the mother's statement), but a partner in the play. In this construction of the meaning field, Mina also emerges as an observer of Yuko's speech. Unlike the meaning construction in Excerpt 1.2, this process is led by Mina and is more dynamic in its proceedings. Here again, Mina's position in relation to her mother as the one who knows the children in hoi-kuen well appears in the succession of differentiations in the field of meaning.

These analyses of the two excerpts from the perspective of meanacting, focusing on the dialectic nature of meaning, exemplify the process by which a variety of information concerning self and others (relating to each other) emerges to form a configuration. It can be described as a realization of the dialectic dynamics that signs have. This also clarifies the perspective of the participants who introduce new meaning, and the positioning in the conversation is achieved in the successive differentiations of the meaning field that they share. Activities in hoikuen—institutional contexts in which many children interact with each other—offer concepts to describe, or frames to look at, other people (e.g., roles in pretend play), though they do not always develop into ontogenesis that offers a stable perspective for self and others. The next section will apply this framework to the other mother-child pair (Yuuma corpus) and further elaborate the understanding of this process.

How Concepts Work Together to Construct a Configuration: An Analysis of Yuuma's Stories

In the analyses above, we observed many different types of concepts working in conversation to form configurations of children who have common futures and differences. Using these concepts, Mina enumerated some of her friends in order to construct a grid to position herself. As I discussed, enumeration of children observed is one natural way of understanding experience, because of the basic feature of hoikuen whereby many same-aged children gather. In the Yuuma corpus, in which 89 episodes of conversation mention his friends and himself in yochien (another type of institution for young children), a variety of concepts concerning membership (e.g., belonging to various groups in the yochien, close friendships) or personal characteristics (e.g., abilities, characteristic behaviors) appeared. These also worked to interrelate Yuuma and others in conversations, often accompanying their enumeration. In the following sections, I will attempt an analysis focusing on examples utilizing group membership as a foundational frame in which to place children.

Although it depends on the policy of each institution or school, we can observe many types of activities in which children participate as groups formed of several members (ordinarily four to six children) at hoikuen, yochien, and elementary schools in Japan. These groups are designated by numbers or names for identification. The children in each group often sit together to eat lunch and are expected to do their activities collaboratively. In the conversation with Yuuma, his mother often asked how they ate lunch, with group membership used as a frame to position the children. To describe how the concepts at yochien work in meaning construction leading to the emergence of presentational self, I introduce three episodes of conversation observed in different periods of recording.

Excerpt 3.3
(Komatsu, 2013, pp. 123–124, Excerpt 1, cited with minor modifications)

[After talking about the seating arrangement for lunch at yochien.]

1. Mo: [I] see. (1 s) Then everyone says "Itadakimasu," [ritual greeting chorus before meal] don't you?
2. Yu: Yes. (3 s) [We] selected a group [of children who lead the greeting] for lunch, before.
3. Mo: Eh? Is there such a group for lunch?
4. Yu: Yes, [there are] the star group, the watermelon [group] and the [speaking simultaneously with line 5] tulip
5. Mo: Yucchi [nickname for Yuuma], what group [do you] belong to?
6. Yu: The melon [group] is next to the strawberry [group] xx [inaudible, laughs].
7. Mo: Eh? Is your group strawberry [group]?
8. Yu: Yeah, yeah.
9. Mo: Who belongs to strawberry? [Do you] remember now? (1 s)
10. Yu: Kentaro [Yuuma's friend, boy], Rina [Yuuma's friend, girl], (Yes) Minori [Yuuma's friend girl] (Yes)
11. Mo: And [speaking simultaneously with line 12] Yucchi? (Yes) Five [children]?
12. Yu: Just [five] Yeah.
13. Yu: Yes. (1 s)
14. Mo: Kentaro, Yucchi, Minori (1 s), Rina? (Yes) and Yucchi.
15. Yu: Yeah. (1 s) Say, mom.
16. Mo: What?
17. Yu: Kentaro.
18. Mo: Kentaro.
19. Yu: Yucchi.
20. Mo: Yucchi. (1 s)
21. Yu: xx [inaudible]
22. Mo: Rina.
23. Yu: Minori.
24. Mo: Minori. (3 s)
25. Yu: Four [children]?
26. Mo: But here, just four children. Why?

Yuuma is 5/9 years old.

Yuuma started attending the yochien when he was 4 years and 11 months old and Excerpt 3.3 was recorded at the end of Yuuma's first year there. In this episode of conversation, his mother is asking about the way they ate lunch, and Yuuma introduces the names of the groups (line 4). Answering his mother's request (line 9), he describes with whom he makes up the "strawberry" group (line 10). The conversation continues with the mother confirming the group's membership, based on her understanding that the group is formed of five children (line 11). The configuration of children including Yuuma himself resembles what I discussed earlier as the meaning construction from Excerpt 1.2, because it is the simple enumeration of children without further development. However, the details of this interaction are different:

that is, the groups are clearly introduced by Yuuma (line 4). The relationship between Yuuma and his mother is also slightly different from the positioning observed in Excerpt 1.2. The mother asks questions repeatedly to lead the conversation, focusing on group membership. However, Yuuma also assumes a position to impart his knowledge by asking his mother to repeat the names of his friends (lines 15–24).

Thus, this is also an example of the emergence of presentational self in the configuration of the child and others, and it shows the role of concepts used in the activities that children experience. Later in the recordings, as discussed when comparing Excerpts 1.2 and 3.2, Yuuma and his mother show variations of this simple meaning construction (Excerpt 3.4).

Excerpt 3.4
(Komatsu, 2013, pp. 125–127, Excerpt 2, cited with modifications)

[After talking about Yuuma's friend who is slow at eating lunch.]

1 Mo: Then [you] eat [lunch]? (1 s) [Do you] eat lunch with members of the *han* [an old-fashioned expression meaning "group"]? (Yeah) Lunch with [members of] the *han*?

2 Yu: Yeah, what does *han* mean?

3 Mo: Oh. [Do you] eat with [members of] the group? (Yes) Sorry, sorry. With the group?

4 Yu: Yes. What does *han* (Yes) mean?

5 Mo: Meaning [of *han*]? Hmm. When I visited [your] class on parents' day, (Yes) you were enjoying origami, (Yeah) sitting with [members of] *han*, weren't you? (Yes) Group. (Yes) Yucchi [nickname for Yuuma] and Yukari [Yuuma's friend, girl] and.

6 Yu: Shinki Kentaro [Yuuma's friend, boy] (Kentaro and) Hiroki [Yuuma's friend, boy] and.

7 Mo: Hiroki and (1 s) who? [speaking simultaneously with line 8] One more child.

8 Yu: Isuzu [Yuuma's friend, girl].

9 Mo: Ah [You] sat next to Isuzu, didn't you? (Yes) And [you] eat together. Fo, five children? Lunch. (Yes) [You] sit and eat in that seat? (Yes) Then, all say "Itadakimasu?" (Yes) And "Gochisosama" [ritual greeting chorus after meal]

10 Yu: [We] didn't use tables today.

11 Mo: [You] didn't use tables today? (No) Why?

12 Yu: Well, coz, tomorrow, today, [we] didn't eat lunch [at yochien].

13 Mo: Ah, [you] set up the tables on the day for lunch?

14 Yu: Yes, yes.

15 Mo: [Do you] set up the tables by yourself? (Yes) Where are the tables [when you're not using them]?

16 Yu: Somewhere beside there, side, um, there is a piano, the piano isn't it? (Yeah, yeah) And right beside there. (Um) Here, here.

17 Mo: [You] keep them here. (xx [inaudible]) And [do you] set them up yourself
       for lunch? (Yes) I see. (1 s)
18 Yu: Yucchi is [I am] a strong boy.
19 Mo: A strong boy? Then, tables, is there a table only for Yucchi or for Hiroki
       [Yuuma's friend, boy]? Is your name on the table? Or, [can you] use any
       table [you want]? (Yes) Tables.
20 Yu: Yeah, the tallest [of the children] is at the front. (Um) And smaller children
       in the back. (Um) Small, small, small.
21 Mo: Ah, Yucchi [you] sit there because [you're] the tallest? (Yeah) Ah, I see I
       see. (1 s) What was [your] job [in class] today, Yucchi? (2 s)
22 Yu: [I] don't have any job today, today.
23 Mo: Oh, [you] didn't have a job.
23 Yu: Yo-chan [Yuuma's friend, girl] [did].
24 Mo: Yo-chan had a job?
25 Yu: Yes, Yo-chan and her group.
26 Mo: Group? So, [you] didn't have any job today?
27 Yu: No. (1 s) Take turns. (Eh?) Take turns.
28 Mo: Ah, [you] take turns. (Um) What kind of jobs are there? (2 s)
29 Yu: [Shall I] tell you? (Yes) (2 s) The cherry flowers [group], (3 s) the butterfly
       (Yeah), (3 s) the strawberry (Um) the cherry, (Um) and the tulip.
30 Mo: Oh, are these the names of the groups? (Yes) So, what kind of jobs do these
       groups have?

                                                          Yuuma is 6/0 years old.

   This interaction was observed in Yuuma's second year at yochien. In the long
flow of interaction, the subject of conversation moves in relation to the activities he
experienced in the classroom. Throughout this move, the subjects always have some
relationship to the group he belongs to. After enumerating the members of his group
(his mother uses "*han*" in Japanese) (lines 5–8), Yuuma mentions the table he regularly uses with no clear relationship to his mother's questions (lines 9–10). In this
interaction, Yuuma extends the field of meaning from his list of friends to the specific episode of the day. Adopting the terms of meanacting, this represents the development of meaning in the **non-A** field in relation to the elaboration of group
membership—i.e., field **A**—in the former interaction.
   Although the meaning construction after this turn was led by the mother (lines
11–17), this also works to introduce his perspective into the conversation. He again
introduces the topic "Yucchi is a strong boy" (line 18) in relation to the set-up of
tables for lunch. In this way, Yuuma clarifies his unique perspective in relation to his
mother's during the description of the groups in terms of members, usage of tables,
seating arrangements, and jobs assigned. This meaning construction also extends
into Yuuma's physical strength and height. Thus, Yuuma at yochien becomes clear
through multiple comparisons and descriptions here to observers.
   These two episodes of conversation by Yuuma and his mother follow the process
I discussed in the case of Mina and her mother. Activities children experience offer
frames in which to place children and construct who the child (Mina or Yuuma) was,

though this activates by chance. This configuration has the potential for further development from a simple enumeration of names to the description of a variety of characteristics, and this is another aspect of the positioning that the child and the mother achieve through interaction. Thus, the presentational self emerges in multiple relationships in which a child is associated with others. Further, as the next example shows, it can include a very personal aspect of relationships.

Enumeration Shifts to the Personal

Excerpt 3.5 was recorded during Yuuma's last term at yochien. As in the two episodes introduced above, this interaction begins with the mother's questioning about his experiences during lunchtime (line 1), to which Yuuma answers by enumerating his friends (line 2). From this arrangement, the mother introduces an affectionate relationship between Yuuma and a girl (Sayaka) and asks the reason why he likes her (line 5). Not answering this question, her son introduces an episode of his friend's kissing the same girl (line 6). This exemplifies that the framework to enumerate or compare children extends into the framework used to describe more personal or private aspects of relationships. In other words, it shows the broad range of meaning construction that starts from group membership.

This development of meaning also brings about a positive mood for the child and his mother—that is, the shift of the topic to the personal, somewhat romantic, aspect of interpersonal relationships enables the mother to poke fun at Yuuma's luck in a new group (line 11). Although she returns to confirming Yuuma's good relations (lines 15 and 17) at yochien, the meaning construction here enables the playful *teasing* in conversation that is not evident in Excerpts 3.3 or 3.4.

Excerpt 3.5
(Komatsu, 2013, pp. 128–129, Excerpt 3, cited with modifications)

1 Mo: Wait a minute. Sorry, sorry. [Let's go back to] What [we] talked about just now. (Yes) With whom [did you] eat lunch today?

2 Yu: Sayaka [Yuuma' friend, girl] was next to Yucchi [nickname for Yuuma] here. (Yes) Shingo [Yuuma's friend, boy], Nana [Yuuma's friend, girl] here, Shingo was next to Nana, and Ayumi [Yuuma's friend, girl] was next to Shingo.

3 Mo: Ah, [you ate] with [members of] your *han*. With members of the group.

4 Yu: Yes. Group.

5 Mo: xx [inaudible] (Yes) So, next to Yucchi is Sayaka. (Yes) Your sweetheart, Sayaka! (Yes) Yucchi [You] love her, don't you? (Yes) Sayaka. (Yes) Why [do you] love her?

6 Yu: Shinta [Yuuma's friend, boy], er, (Yes) has smooched with Sayaka once.

7 Mo: Really? Didn't Sayaka refuse that? (No) (1 s) Ah. (2 s) I see. Who [do you] like the most, Yucchi? (2 s)

 8 Yu: xx [inaudible], Sayaka and (Yes) Takai Ma-kun [Yuuma's friend, boy] (Yes). Takai Ma-kun and (Yes) (4 s)
 9 Mo: Then, just the kids you like! The new group. (Yes) Girls.
10 Yu: Yes [speaking simultaneously with line 11] and,
11 Mo: Hey. And Nana too! (Yes) Wow!
12 Yu: So, Takai Ma-kun belongs to the ice group.
13 Mo: Ma-kun is in the ice group?
14 Yu: Not in (Yes) xx [inaudible] group.
15 Mo: Hum, is there a quarrel in the group? Yucchi.
16 Yu: [We] don't.
17 Mo: [Are you] good friends? (Yes)

Yuuma is 6/8 years old.

The characteristics of the meaning construction here, in comparison with Excerpts 3.3 and 3.4, may derive from Yuuma and his mother's understanding of others at yochien. However, just as with the corpus of Mina and her mother, such an episode is rare in the recordings and thus is not considered a simple reflection of stable knowledge concerning them. Although the concepts that children encounter at yochien or hoikuen often work as the foundation for setting out the names of the children concerned, how meaning construction and positioning between the participants develop from such a configuration will depend on the unpredictable dialectic dynamics of **A <> non-A** that our use of signs introduces into the field of meaning.

Conclusion

Our conversations in natural settings are not only for transmission of what we know to others, but for our relationship-making and our making sense of past and future. This is also true for young children and their mothers. In addition to this hybrid nature, interaction in conversation is always affected by its environment at the micro- and macro- levels. Fluctuation of conversation in natural settings due to this complicated architecture makes it difficult to understand the interaction from the perspective of a great deal of research in developmental psychology that presupposes the stability of interactions obtained from the ontogenetic development of children.

In this chapter, by touching on several episodes from such non-stable but rich recordings of mother-child conversations, I have attempted to describe several variations in the emergence of presentational self that developed from the mentioning of others that children encounter in the institutionalized setting. The episodes showed a common foundational configuration of children and differences in development to position the self and others. This resembles the process of listening to an orchestral work unfold, in which one simple theme develops through variation and by adding instruments.

The presentational self appears as a configuration of self and others, and the examples of conversation have showed that this configuration is constructed using a variety of categories or concepts that children encounter in their lives. Within the framework by Josephs, Valsiner, and Surgan (1999), I hypothetically described the process by which one of these categories sets a latent field for further meaning in relation to a preceding description of self or others. In other words, the self emerges through the power of signs that provides us the possibility of developing new meaning from existing meaning. As the examples discussed here are necessarily limited in number and characteristics, there might be other episodes of conversation in which we can find other types of presentational self. However, at least in the examples I analyzed, the presentational self is what becomes observable through the participants' actions in this possibility of new meaning. To offer an extreme example of this basic schema, even silence in conversation can possibly be an act of extending shared meaning and can be a place for the presentational self.

Despite this generalizable nature, the genre of conversation I discussed is not so common in the recordings. It is also presumable that children and their mothers will not talk as in these examples if researchers ask them to *replay* the conversations. One reason for this is that conversations develop from over-abundant microgenetic meaning construction. In these works, meaning occasionally develops to present a clear figure of self in relation to others, just as wind waves in the beach are variously distributed in their heights and sometimes very high waves appear. From this perspective, Excerpts 3.3, 3.4, and 3.5 from the Yuuma corpus may be considered as something resembling the highest of multiple repeating waves. Children are always engaging in meaning construction but this does not necessarily signify the permanent emergence of clear presentational self in the conversation.

In other words, the discussion here is of an understanding that considers the self that appears locally and momentarily in our active relationships with physical and interpersonal surroundings, and via the functioning of signs. To clarify this framework further, I will compare it with existing approaches to the self in psychology in the next chapter.

Chapter 4
Rethinking the Frameworks of Psychology: What the Self Was and What it Was Not in Developmental Psychology

> The *great* snare of the psychologist is the *confusion of his own standpoint with that of the mental fact* about which he is making his report.
>
> James, W. (1890, p. 196)

Throughout the history of psychology as an independent science, there have been many investigations concerning *the self*. Beginning from a deep, ascetic reflection by researchers themselves, *"Who am I?,"* which has its roots in philosophical thinking, the main focus of psychological arguments is now upon the question, *"Who are you?"*—i.e., how can we understand the self of study participants? Developing many derivative concepts and a variety of methods, researchers exuberantly and confidently insist that they *can* understand *our* selves, not theirs. What researchers also aim for is to explain our behavior or our adjustment by means of terms containing the prefix "self-"—for example, self-evaluation or self-worth—and they sometimes indicate ways of looking at ourselves considered desirable.

The theoretical framework of the presentational self, introduced in the foregoing chapters, also attempts to construct our understanding of others. However, it does not depend on the pairing of questions from researchers with answers from study participants. It carefully describes what is occurring in the process of meaning construction and the effect this has on observers who look at the process with analytic intent. This schema is important to avoid the psychologists' fallacy that James (1890) warned of, in which we confuse what we understand with what we are going to describe. In this chapter, I first point out that our understanding of others, including self-representation, is *our* post hoc meaning construction from *their* meaning construction. With this understanding, I describe the fundamental principle of the presentational self, and discuss the methodological implications of the framework in relation to existing studies concerning the selves of children.

© The Author(s) 2019
K. Komatsu, *Meaning-Making for Living*, SpringerBriefs in Psychology,
https://doi.org/10.1007/978-3-030-19926-5_4

The Complex of Perspectives and Methods for Understanding Children's Selves

Methods of psychological research are always accompanied by assumptions about the mind, and psychological inquiries into the self also rely on several presuppositions about what the self is, even if not a formal definition. To understand children's selves, which are also the object of my inquiry, researchers have developed rating scales consisting of items asking children about their lives or what they think of themselves (e.g., "I can do things as well as most other people"; Marsh, Smith, & Barnes, 1985). In contrast with these attempts to represent children's selves by quantitative indices, other researchers have used open questions such as: "What kind of person are you?" or "What are you especially proud of about yourself?" (Damon & Hart 1988, p. 81). Children's answers to these questions are classified into categories to show the "evidence" concerning the development of self-understanding.

These approaches share assumptions in common with a great deal of other psychological research. They focus on the self as an internal entity that is clarified through study participants' reflections triggered by questions posed by researchers (e.g., items in questionnaires, questions in interviews). We consider children's ratings or their answers to researchers' questions not as their evasion of examination, but a manifestation of what they maintain as their representations. Thus, the existing methods for understanding children's selves—that is, self-representation or self-understanding—serve to restrict what children's selves can be. It must be *inside* us and comparable among children in one occasion, and also stable in the flow of time. Historically, these assumptions have their origins partially in the dawning age of psychology, as in the definition by James (1890),[1] who compared the self with our possessions. And contemporaneously, they work to bring about the legitimacy of psychological measurement and its usefulness for prediction. (For instance, appropriate self-understanding works as a foundation for better vocational selection.)

On these academic foundations, research supports a socially approved belief concerning child development and education, which aims at fostering children's self-understanding and self-evaluation. Maintaining children's adequate confidence in their own selves and nurturing appropriate self-understanding are considered indispensable aspects of children's social development. Working from a comprehensive understanding concerning the development of children's selves, researchers often recommend interventions for children who show self-evaluation or self-understanding that deviates from the standard. For example, Harter (1999) offered detailed explanations concerning the characteristics of children's self-representation in each developmental period, also indicating some points requiring attention for effective

---

[1] James (1890) defined *self*, or *me*, "*In its widest possible sense*, however, *a man's Self is the sum total of all that he CAN call his*" (p. 291)

interventions.[2] Supporting these recommendations, diverse educational efforts to promote children's self-understanding and respect their sense of self-worth are not limited to academics or educators but also provided to ordinary parents through many websites.[3] In this way, our society considers school education a social apparatus for the development and elaboration of children's selves, and psychology and school education function as an academic-institutional *complex* that exerts an undeniable system of values on our viewing of children's selves.

The Self is From Twofold Meaning Construction

In contrast to the academic presupposition that children's answers to the standardized questions reflect their internal entities with some level of measurement error, we can see these answers as the results of participants' meaning construction that is triggered by the questions posed by researchers. When we ask children "Who are you?," we often expect them to define themselves using social categories or socially shared standards for evaluation, which also leads to their actions (Fig. 4.1). For example, when children describe themselves as "good at mathematics," this is considered to reflect their positive evaluations of themselves related to their everyday conduct, although their answers are not necessarily precise descriptions of

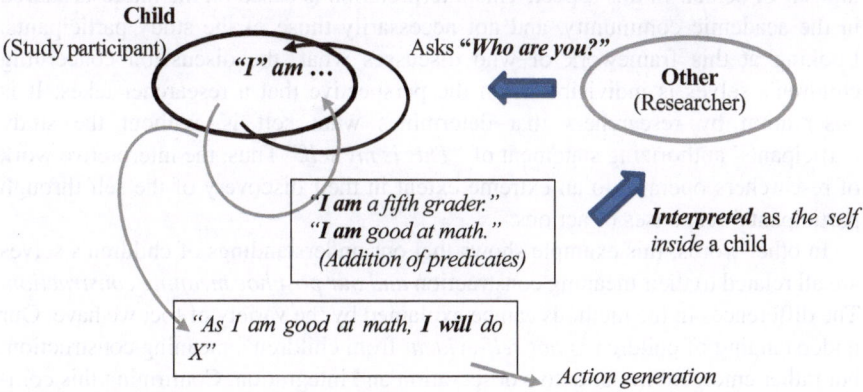

Fig. 4.1 The process of a child's answer to the question, "Who are you?"

---

[2] I do not insist on total abolition of these tests. Even if a standardized test shows the self clarified through the concern of researchers, educators, and policy makers, tests can serve as a viable and fair option for coping with the pressure to *prove* the efficiency of efforts, in the current social circumstances that require authoritative evidence to underpin educational efforts. However, it must be noted that this is a different type of meaning construction for children, compared with the meaning construction we observe in daily life.

[3] For example, "10 ways to nurture your child's self-concept" (http://calm4kids.org/10-ways-to-nurture-your-childs-self-concept/)

themselves. Actually, it is in this process that the self or the subject *"I"* becomes emergent, seeking for answers that are valid in the relationships between children and researchers.

When we are asked a question, it is open to many possible reactions, including ignoring the question. If we decide to present an answer considering the context, we explore a variety of possible answers and select one that suits the context well. When we think of our academic abilities, for example, we do not suddenly leap into a decision such as, "I am good at mathematics." Such a description is already the result of social exchanges in the past: i.e., questions from parents, comments from friends, and so forth. After such a trigger, we may re-construct our experiences in math class with boring emotions, confusion about difficult tasks, or sometimes pride in overtaking our friends. We can also see the self that works in such processes of constructing answers in the possible field of meaning construction and makes a position in relation to the question.

Research into developmental psychology has not focused on the process of meaning construction but only picked up the results of this process. However, the self-representation clarified through this process is the researchers' post hoc understanding of what children have constructed in relation to the interests of others. In other words, children's answers to researchers' questions are *interpreted* to become their "self-representation." For example, a child's statement "I am popular" in response to the question "What kind of person are you?" is cognizant that he or she has prior concerns in interpersonal relationships and keeps a positive view of himself or herself in this aspect. This interpretation is based on the interests shared in the academic community, and not necessarily those of the study participants. Looking at this framework of who discusses what, the discussion concerning children's selves is indivisible from the perspective that a researcher takes. It is observation by researchers that determines what self is, without the study participants' authorizing statement of *"This is my self."* Thus, the interpretive work of researchers operates to an extreme extent in their discovery of the self through participants' responses or actions.

In other words, this example shows that our understandings of children's selves are all related to their meaning construction *and our post hoc meaning construction.* The differences in the methods can be explained by the variety of foci we have. Our understanding of children is *not self-evident* from children's meaning construction, but rather emergent in our active observation and integration. Confirming this common nature concerning our understanding of children's selves, I will describe unique perspectives that the framework of presentational self offers in the next section.

Formalizing the Presentational Self: Three Perspectives

Perspective on the interaction observed in children's lives Although questions in the standardized methods can trigger children's meaning construction as I discussed above, we must consider the non-ubiquity of the reflections that these methods demand. In children's lives, they may rarely understand themselves in relation to a set of standardized questions. Items on standardized tests compress the complex processes children engage in life—not only in the content of reflection, but also in the needs of reflection—into one short sentence and ratings on a five- or seven-point scale.

There is another type of approach for young children's selves. Some studies have analyzed conversations in which young children and their family members talk about the children's experiences commencing when the children were around 2 years old. These studies focused on developmental changes in the structure of narratives, or the content of the conversations, with a special focus on children's autobiographical memories that is closely related to the development of self-understanding (see Nelson & Fivush 2004, for review). In most of these studies, researchers directly asked children and their mothers to talk about topics compatible with their standards. With this method, they had the recordings of conversations that were comparable to each other in content and construction. However, as in many standardized tests, the meaning construction occurring in this process by children and mothers was also based on the researchers' interests.

In reality, the site in which children accomplish reflection is not the specific situation of testing, but their somewhat whimsical interactions with others around them. Children reflect on what they did and whom they met: that is to say, joys, troubles, or other miscellaneous issues. What we see there is not only garrulous talk with rich imagery of themselves, but short and sharp-witted utterances about their experiences, or, as I mentioned in the previous chapter, even complete silence in the flow of interaction can show their unique perspectives and "who they were." This leads to our understanding that one sincere way to understand children's selves is, if the child is young, to observe and interpret their ways of *presenting* their experiences in very ordinary situations in their lives. Although this orientation works at the cost of reproducibility and comparability of the data, it can reduce interference by the researchers' intentions and enables observation of a wide variety of children's meaning construction in natural settings.

Perspective on the self emerging in relationships From the beginning of my analysis, I focused on two types of interpersonal relationships in which we find the emergence of self: the interpersonal relationships described in the conversation and the interpersonal relationship between the child and the partner in conversation. Although they are always on the move, a fundamental system can be described as in Fig. 4.2.

First, the configuration of the child (e.g., Mina or Yuuma) and his or her friends that is constructed in the shared field of meaning construction is described as **A** in Fig. 4.2 below. As I discussed in Chap. 2 (see Fig. 2.2), the shared field of meaning also involves future infinity and past infinity. In the process of conversation, a variety of concepts or episodes are introduced to clarify the commonalities and differences among children and to construct a configuration of them. Even if the child does not describe himself or herself, the perspective from which he or she describes

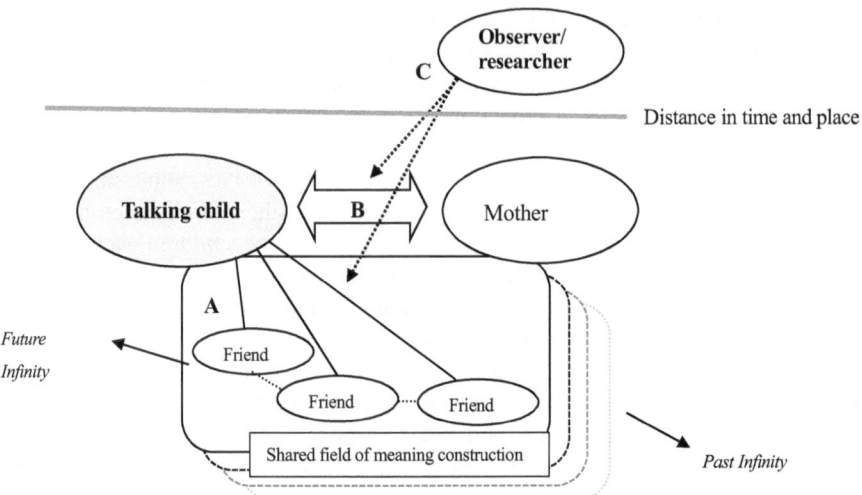

Fig. 4.2 Basic framework of the presentational self (Cited with modifications from Komatsu (2012, p. 359, Figure 1))

his or her friends becomes clear in the meaning construction, thus locating the child in the configuration.

Second, this description is also the process of constructing a relationship between the child and the partner in the conversation (**B** in Fig. 4.2). As we saw in the examples of conversation, the mother also contributes to the construction of the configuration in which her child is situated, and the field of meaning construction (the rectangle in Fig. 4.2) also depends on the mother. In this interaction, the child can also assume a position. For example, Mina made use of her right to assume a position to teach her mother about the children, as the events in hoikuen are what she experienced. On the other hand, when the topic is something the mother knows well, as in Excerpt 1.1 in which the child confirms that she was a cute baby, the relationship between the child and the mother becomes different and the mother assumes a position to clarify past events. Thus, the positioning between the child and his or her mother becomes clear in close relationship with their co-construction of the field of meaning.

Third, the analysis of the conversation I presented in the foregoing chapters entails the active observer who constructs and finds the presentation of the child in two types of relationship (A and B) through conversation. This is accomplished across the spatial and temporal distance between the site of conversation and the analysis (**C** in Fig. 4.2). As was discussed in the previous section, this is our post hoc meaning construction from the traces of meaning construction developed in the conversation.

Perspective on the self as presentation, not representation In existing studies analyzing conversations between young children and their family members, researchers supposed that autobiographical memory is both constructed in the conversation *and* explains what is talked about in the conversation. Nelson (2003) used the terms *narrative self-understanding* (3–6 years of age) and *cultural self-understanding* (5–7 years) to describe what are constructed in these conversations. In other words, the process of conversation is supposed to be related to the *representations* children have and they explain the same types of actions in the resembling settings.

Our perspective described here conceptualizes the self in a different way. The framework abandons the idea of self as representation somehow inside children and considers the self a *presentation* that becomes clear through the complex arrangement described in Fig. 4.2. Though differing from the widespread presuppositions of modern psychology, the philosophical discussion concerning self tells us that presupposing the self as an entity is *not* an undeniable truth. According to Metzinger (2011), there is a variety of possible understandings of the self, including the *no-self alternative*. In other words, "there seems to be no empirical evidence and no truly convincing conceptual argument that supports the actual existence of 'a' self" (Metzinger, 2011, p. 279). From this viewpoint, psychologists' assumptions about the self are based only on intuitive soundness: that is, on commonsense (Komatsu, 2012).

Modalities of Understanding Children's Selves

Although I have offered a theoretical framework of the presentational self featuring its uniqueness in relation to existing research into developmental psychology, it still has commonalities with the majority of psychological methods and thinking, if we take the view that all these psychological methods use the *traces* of meaning construction by children. From this perspective, our understanding of children's selves is always our *post-factum reconstruction* from their meaning construction as I discussed above. To clarify this point and elaborate the framework, I describe the modalities of understanding children's selves (Table 4.1). Further, in this comparison, I introduce our understanding of the self *on site* for describing the nature of psychological data.

Understanding of children's selves from the result of meaning construction This is the most frequently used approach for understanding children's selves. As I discussed in the first part of this chapter, many studies use questionnaires or interviews, presuming that the self is an entity that is available for the meta-cognitive reflection needed for any response to such questions. In these studies, children's selves are presented as aggregated scores derived from ratings (e.g., scores of self-esteem measures) or the summaries of answers in interviews that are categorized into several groups (e.g., academic ability, outward appearance, personality characteristics, and more). The same applies to the analysis of mother-child conversations about their past experiences when researchers attempt to describe conversations using several concepts to summarize the characteristics of interaction. For example, researchers used the frequency of children or parents mentioning "internal states" or the extent to which they

Table 4.1 Modalities of understanding children's selves

Mode of understanding	Data used	Researchers' *post hoc* meaning constructions concerning the self
Understanding from the *result* of meaning construction	Static configuration of several indices	Describing the stable self (e.g., self-understanding, self-evaluation) inside children
	Bearing no relationship in time and totally detached from context	Comparison of results from other children or other instances
	No consideration of the relationships or the contexts in which data are produced	Open to a variety of understandings concerning the process children had in self-representation as described in the assessment
		(very open but fallacious)
Understanding from the *process* of meaning construction	Recordings of interaction or narratives that maintain the change in time and relational nature	Figuring out the self that emerges in meaning construction
		Understanding of relational achievements
	Data are specific to time and space	A variety of interpretations and understandings of interaction are possible
		(open and relative)
⇕		
Understanding *on site*	One time only and embedded in unique background	Impossible for a third person and possible only for the person concerned **(genuine but closed)**
	Microgenesis of meaning in ongoing experiences	

introduced new information into the conversation to figure out what happened in the conversation (see Nelson & Fivush 2004; Fivush, Haden, & Reese, 2006, for review). These are also accumulations of fragmented pieces of interaction.

These methods describe a configuration of elements (e.g., scores on standardized measurements, numbers of each type of answer in open-ended interviews), but they do not suppose how these meaning constructions were achieved. They also ignore many types of relationships created by researchers and study participants. When children are confronted with a questionnaire, they have a variety of possible reactions, though these are almost invisible. Some of them will be interested in what happens in the course of research, but for others these are boring tasks. Some children may become anxious about what the test is assessing. After these encounters, children commence their meaning construction to answer the questionnaire items. In most studies concerning mother-child conversations, participants who are asked to talk about their experiences have a variety of reactions, as it is actually very unnatural to be *asked* to talk on specific topics.

The very composition of this genre of data makes it easy to construct, reproduce, and sometimes fabricate them. These data are also quite open to a variety of post hoc meaning construction because they are questions paired with simple answers, independent of the context of real lives. Researchers can construct *their* stories to explain why children answer in a certain way. However, these post hoc meaning constructions often depend on the knowledge or orientation of whoever is reading the data. This openness can also lead to mistaken understandings, and this disadvantage becomes prominent when constructed from data fabricated to make a positive impression on observers (e.g., fake ratings in a questionnaire).[4]

In these attempts, fixed stimuli for this meaning construction (e.g., items in questionnaires) are considered to guarantee the objectivity of the results and enable us to compare the profiles of multiple children. Using the framework given in Fig. 4.2, I illustrate this process as in Fig. 4.3 below.

As Valsiner (2017) pointed out, research becomes possible by constructing a shared field of meaning between researchers and participants who construct their identities in the move to their *meeting place*. Questionnaires and interviews are examples of such shared fields, and these are also the sites where researchers and participants negotiate their positions, as I described above for children's encounters with questionnaires. Participants construct meaning here in relation to the items shown to them—that is, their answers to questionnaires are in the ways they interact with items (**A**) *and* the other people conducting the research (**B**). However, research-ers ignore these dynamics or this context, due to the fact that they use standardized, common questions and move to a position from which they appear to look only at the results of meaning construction as what shows children's selves (e.g., self-understanding), independent of context (**C**, see the upward movement of the researcher in Fig. 4.3). This shows that standardized methods of psychology are

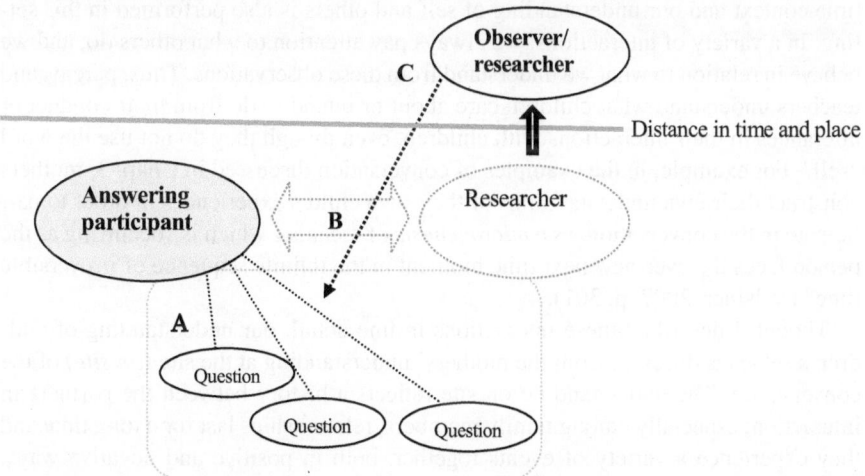

Fig. 4.3 Procedure of psychological assessment by standardized methods (Cited with modifications from Komatsu (2012, p. 362, Figure 2))

---

[4]This resembles the urge to take impressive pictures for social media in order to be perceived as happy or successful. Ease of construction and openness to meaning construction are at the foundation of this.

organized in disregard of many aspects of relationships, shown by dotted lines in Fig. 4.3, that were actually involved in the process of research.

Understanding of children's selves from the process of meaning construction In contrast with the simple framework of standardized methods described above, recordings of what children do or say are basically organized fragments cut from a flow of time, and they typically maintain the relationships among children's behaviors (or sayings) in time.

Although narratives can be total fraud with no concrete foundation in children's lives, they all are meaning constructions and we can attempt post hoc meaning constructions from these data. The framework of the presentational self is based on such process-inclusive data and is a stance inclusive of the dynamics at work in meaning construction. However, because the data are only extracts from daily lives, they are also open to other interpretations. Figuring out the selves in recorded conversations is possible in post hoc meaning construction but my discussion is not necessarily an *absolute* one, and our post hoc meaning constructions concerning individual interactions often compete with each other. In other words, the presentation of our experiences or understandings is open and involves relativity, as it is detached from specific context. For this reason, we must consider the understanding of children's selves on site discussed below and distinguish it from our post hoc understanding.

Understanding of children's selves on site Understanding of children's selves is not limited to research in psychology. Our experiences are embedded in a unique, one-time context and our understanding of self and others is also performed in this setting. In a variety of interactions, we always pay attention to what others do, and we behave in relation to what we understand from these observations. Thus, parents and teachers understand what children care about or intend to do from their conduct or utterances in their interactions with children, even though they do not use the word "self." For example, in the examples of conversation discussed in Chap. 3, mothers construct their own understandings of their own child's experiences in order to participate in the conversation, as a *microgenesis* of meaning which is "occurring as the person faces the ever-new next time moment in the infinite sequence of irreversible time" (Valsiner, 2007, p. 301).

Though I described these interactions in fine detail, our understanding of children's selves is different from the mothers' understanding at the site (*on site*) of the conversation. The understanding on site reflects a history between the partners in interaction; especially among family members, relationships last for a long time and they experience a variety of events together, both in positive and negative ways. When Mina and her mother talk about their visit to a zoo in the past (Except 1.1), what a particular zoo may represent is different for them and for us. The mothers' and children's semiotic processes required to understand the partner on site work in relationship with complex affective reactions that are the results of these past experiences. Thus, understanding of others on site is embedded in context in multiple ways, and of course it has a subjective nature: i.e., *closed* to researchers. We can ask mothers to look back and narrate their understanding of their children in the conversation, but these stories are already different from their understanding that has been at work in the conversation.

If we convert this understanding of others into the understanding of ourselves on site, this mode corresponds with the following discussion from Mead (1934).

> The "I" is the response of the organism to the attitudes of the others; the "me" is the organized set of attitudes of others which one himself assumes. The attitudes of the others constitute the organized "me," and then one reacts toward that as an "I." (p. 175)

When we modify the schema of the presentational self into the model of *our* construction of ourselves, in which an interacting person himself or herself takes the position to find his or her behavior from the viewpoint of an assumed other, it constructs a feedback loop to clarify the self as "me" in relation to the acting "I" (Fig. 4.4).

In this example, the distance between the shared field of meaning construction (the big rectangle) and who observes it disappears. When we interact with objects or others (**A**), we assume somewhat *generalized* others and an "organized set of attitudes" (**B**). What is also working in this process is the "I" that is constituting "me" in the process and creating reactions to others' responses (**C**). Although heavily transformed from the original form in Fig. 4.2, this shows that the characteristics of the framework that describes how we find our self through interaction are also related to the idea of the presentational self.

Fig. 4.4 A description of self-perception as performed on site (Cited with modifications from Komatsu (2012, p. 363, Figure 3))

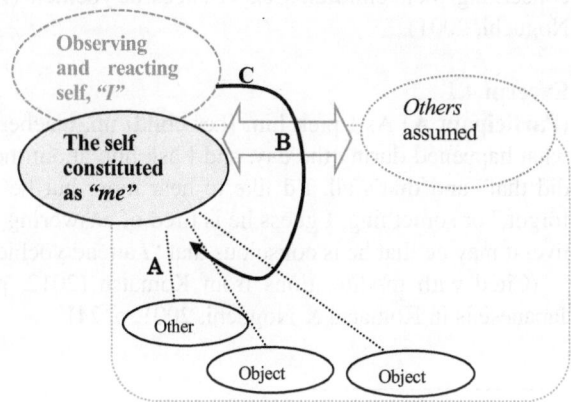

Comparing Understandings of Children's Selves

Table 4.1 shows the gap between psychological understandings of the self and the understanding of the self on site. First, in my discussion here, children's or their family members' understandings of children's selves are based on their understanding on site, while psychological understandings are usually derived from the meaning construction by children detached from context, even when recorded in detail. Two types of psychological understanding are also different from each other.

Researchers use standardized methods in which interactions are restricted and contexts are ignored, because of the presupposition that the self is individual and stable in time. For example, in the studies of conversations between young children and their parents, individual differences in parental elaboration are considered important for the construction of the children's detailed autobiographical memories and related to their understanding of self and others (e.g., their performance in the false belief task) (Fivush et al., 2006). In these approaches, understanding children's selves from the result of meaning construction is useful when believed to work toward favorable development of children. Despite this possible practical utility, this is merely one perspective for viewing children's selves.

The contrasts of these multiple understandings are observable in the meaning of silence in conversation, which I touched upon in the foregoing section. Keeping silent after a question from researchers usually means *no data* in interviews or questionnaires that attempt to construct understanding from the results of meaning construction, and data from such participants is often excluded before final analysis. However, as we also experience in our own conversations, silence serves as a powerful tool for meaning construction in relationships. Mothers who talk with their children actually feel this in their interactions. Excerpts 4.1 and 4.2 are from interviews[5] that asked mothers of 3 year-old children about their daily conversations concerning their children's experiences at yochien (Komatsu, 2012; Komatsu & Noguchi, 2001).

Excerpt 4.1
(Participant A) As I pick him [her child] up, teachers tell us some stories about what happened during the day, and I ask him about them. He just says, "Yeah, we did that" and that's all. I'd like to hear more but he says, "[I] don't know," "[I] forgot," or something. I guess he is tired of answering, or rather, from his perspective, it may be that he is conscious that "*I* attend yochien, not mom."[6]

(Cited with modifications from Komatsu (2012, p. 364, Excerpt 1), original Japanese is in Komatsu & Noguchi, 2001, p. 74)

---

[5] Original recordings and transcripts are in Japanese. Translations into English were made by the author.

[6] In the original utterance in Japanese, the mother says "It may be because he had a consciousness that the *yochien* is mine." The translation shown in Excerpt 4.1 was determined with the help of native English speakers, to keep the nuance of what the mother was intending (Komatsu, 2012).

Excerpt 4.2

(Participant C) Of course, I'd like to know his behavior or his habits [at yochien], sure. But I feel I shouldn't know them in too much detail. [Several turns omitted] From the day he began to attend yochien, he's been independent from me and has, yeah, his own time and his own relationships, finally. Then, if parents, well, I can't explain it clearly, are over-interested and interfere with their children, I fear it'll be too much for him. [Several turns omitted] Now, he has his friends, there is his teacher, and he says "It's *my* yochien." So I hope he can handle it [the yochien] on his own.

(Cited with modifications from Komatsu (2012, p. 365, Excerpt 2), original Japanese is in Komatsu & Noguchi, 2001, p. 73).

What appears in mothers' understanding of their children's conduct or utterances is considered an appearance of children's uniqueness in relation to their mothers. It can be interpreted as mothers finding out their children's selves in their relationships, as their understanding of their children is described with emphasis on the pronouns "I" and "my" of the child. However, in these excerpts, a mother (Participant A) finds evidence of the development of her son's self in *not* talking much about his experiences. Participant C believes it is important for her to *not* ask about her child's experiences in order to support her child's own style of living, which cannot be shared. Thus, in aspects of daily life, the absence of a detailed story can also clarify or emphasize a child's self. Although the possibility of generalizing these beliefs is unclear, it shows that the self in conversation is never fully grasped by analysis that quantifies what was told there. This example also shows that our focusing on the relational aspects and process of the meaning construction contains the possibility of our edging up to the understanding of children's selves on site, though there remains a qualitative gap that is difficult to overcome.

Conclusion: An *All-Inclusive* Perspective for Children's Selves

The concept of the presentational self is constructed including the process of meaning construction in our relationships, and even entails the observer who discovers the self in the semiotic activities. This orientation might be criticized as neglecting the premise of psychology that a person has some static entity in his or her psyche that can be clarified in objective ways through questioning. As I showed in Fig. 4.3, such standardized methods of psychology ignore some important aspects of our meaning construction that are also at work in children's answering the questions from researchers. Such ignorance is related to their desire for objective and replicable methods of inquiry, and a variety of latent responses of children to the questions are discarded as meaningless.

These can be an approach for our minds, but they are not the only way. The framework of the presentational self deliberately and carefully attempts to include many, if not all, of the elements related to the meaning construction that children attempt in their daily lives. Its process-oriented nature and the inclusion of the observer into the schema render any claim of objectivity difficult, but also enable our access to the complexity and the exquisiteness achieved through the function of signs, as I described in Chap. 3.

After the elaboration of its position in relation to other methods, the next step in developing this theoretical framework is applying it to other instances. For this purpose, I examine elementary school children's stories about their experiences, written as an activity within school education in Japan, from the perspective of the presentational self.

Chapter 5
Construction of Selves Through Written Stories

Although oral storytelling has been investigated in many research areas beyond psychology (e.g., oral history in historical research, the Labovian approach in linguistics), the means for presenting our experiences necessarily include another medium: i.e., written language. Writing one's experiences also involves microgenesis of meaning that is achieved through signs being brought into the writing process. In comparison with what we examined in the analysis of mother-child conversations, the writing process is slower and requires planning. To put it simply, writing is the construction of lines and points in front of us that do not exist in conversation. They are both the traces of the meaning construction for writers and the starting point of meaning construction for readers. Given these characteristics, I consider writing the act of dialogue through a medium that acquires physical form and can be preserved after the dialogue is over.

When young children begin to *write* something by themselves, we often ask what they have drawn or written, connecting each act of drawing or writing with what is signified. Even when they are unclear scribbles, children answer what they mean (Ferreiro, 1985). Thus, from the beginning of our literacy, what we have written works and has meaning in our dialogical interactions, which also implies that what we write always involves a relationship with potential readers. Sometimes we write brief memos or diary entries without expecting interactions with others, but even these usually carry an intention to be read by ourselves in the future.

To extend the coverage of the theoretical framework of the presentational self, here I turn to children's meaning construction achieved through written language with a focus on the *indirect* dialogue in the writings mentioned above. Writings of one's experiences (i.e., diaries) can be a method of psychological inquiry into human development in relation to one's environment (Zittoun & Gillespie, 2012). Based on this fundamental assumption, I focus on the writings of elementary school

© The Author(s) 2019

K. Komatsu, *Meaning-Making for Living*, SpringerBriefs in Psychology,
https://doi.org/10.1007/978-3-030-19926-5_5

children (in third and fourth grade) about their experiences.[1] These writings have been practiced within Japanese school education from its very early period, involving teachers' intentions to promote the development of children's selves. In this inquiry, I will discuss the emergence of children's selves through their acts of writing that works in our social system. The discussion also includes contrasts with the mother-child conversations I discussed in previous chapters.

Children's Writings About Their Experiences in Japanese School Education

In Japanese schools, we can observe many types of children's meaning construction in interactions or activities led by teachers in charge of classes. Among these, especially in elementary schools, there are activities in which children share their experiences with their teachers and classmates. In concrete terms, these activities are called *sakubun* or *tsuzurikata*[2] (composition), *nikki* (diary or journal writing, Fig. 5.1), and *speech* (oral storytelling, Fig. 5.2). Some elementary school teachers set (one of) these activities as a regular task for children in their classes. Children's writings about their experiences analyzed in this chapter are also the result of this habitual task of nikki writing.

The word *nikki* in Japanese is often translated as *diary* in English, but the nature of the writings here are closer to the meaning of the word *journal* in some contexts. It is not a systematic report of events, and children are free to write their experiences, mainly private ones, in their own ways. Concerning this orientation of Japanese teachers toward writing *freely*, Watanabe (2007) suggested that, compared with American or French school education systems, Japanese teachers place more emphasis on the unrestrained expression of children's *subjective* experiences while paying less attention to their technical writing skills (e.g., construction of paragraphs or the appeal of the story). In line with this preference, many Japanese teachers respond through personal reactions or impressions to these stories. Thus, while these are formal activities led by teachers, they are also personalized activities that do not restrict the content or style of writing.

In addition to this unrestricted nature, these activities have been carried out with the intention not only to improve children's academic skills, but also to promote children's development in a broader sense as well-rounded personalities and develop better relationships in classrooms. With this in mind, teachers read children's writ-

---

[1] The discussion in this chapter was developed from the author's collaborative works with Chieri Konno (Komatsu and Konno 2014) and Mako Yamamoto (Yamamoto and Komatsu 2016).

[2] In comparison with sakubun, tsuzurikata is considered a more traditional expression for children's writings or compositions. However, these two words have been used with differing intentions in the history. With the spread of the term sakubun via education reform after World War II, there occurred a broad discussion concerning the differences in meaning of these two words, although no clear definitive conclusion was reached (Sugahara, 2016).

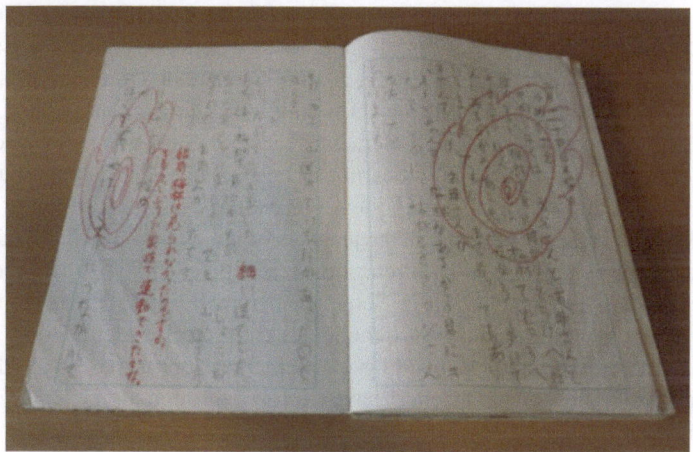

Fig. 5.1 A notebook for writing nikki (fourth grade)
Note: The picture was taken and used with permission

Fig. 5.2 A child gives a speech in front of classmates (fifth grade) (Komatsu, 2012, p. 367, Figure 6)
Note: The picture was taken and used with permission

ings to understand their individuality or personality. A survey by Kajii (2001) that asked elementary school teachers about their perspectives on evaluating sakubun by children showed that they focused not only on children's abilities to construct sentences properly and to craft correct descriptions, but also on the emergence of the unique character or personality of each child. Thus, children's writing work for teachers is a medium for understanding the unique view of each child upon his or her experiences, bearing the characteristic of *non-evaluative* communication in formal school education.

Given these broad but ambiguous objectives, writing nikki is *not* clearly indicated in the official guidelines for the elementary school curriculum issued by MEXT (Ministry of Education, Culture, Sports, Science and Technology), though learning proper compositional writing skills and storytelling are mentioned as goals for children to accomplish through elementary school education. This also means that children engage in these activities not in one standardized fashion but differently depending on each teacher's policy. For example, the frequency of writing personal stories varies depending on the teacher. While writing nikki is usually considered a part of homework for children, some teachers let children write about their private experiences in the classroom. Some teachers will often set a theme for writings but others ask children to choose the topic. Thus, teachers let children write or talk about their experiences depending on their own approaches to children and their objectives. This is what teachers have explored throughout the history of education in Japan.

The Historical Background of Children's Writings About Their Experiences

Although sakubun, tsuzurikata, and nikki indicate different genres of writing in Japan, nikki stories written in elementary school education share many characteristics with sakubun or tsuzurikata. Everyday experiences are the major subject in all these writings and sometimes sakubun or tsuzurikata also includes writings in a daily nikki style. For this reason, here I cover the historical background and the characteristics of sakubun and tsuzurikata education to better understand the relationship between children's writings and their selves as discussed by school teachers.

These activities in which children present their experiences in the school context, in oral or written form, have existed in Japanese elementary schools since the Meiji era (1868–1912), when the modern school system was introduced in Japan. In the first phase of their development, the goal of these activities was not the presentation of personal experiences but rather children clearly describing their thinking or opinions, using classical styles of writing (Namekawa, 1977). However, in the middle of the Meiji era, around 1900, the word *jiko* (meaning "self") appears in relation to the goals of these activities. For example, Namekawa (1977) introduces a discussion in a guide for teachers published in 1891 that insists the main purpose of sakubun writing lies in clear descriptions of one's own thinking, and this discussion already mentions the word jiko. This is surprising because during the Meiji era, ordinary Japanese people had not fully accepted the notion of self as imported from the European tradition. Nevertheless, from the very early period of their development, the premise of these activities was that the self is not a given but instead becomes clearer through work or writing.

In the Taisho era (1912–1926), some teachers began to encourage children to write their personal experiences in colloquial style, following the change of perspectives on children and education known as *jido chushin shugi* (the child-centric education). With this background, a magazine for children was first published in this era (titled *Akai-tori*, in literal translation, Red Bird), and it included a contest of children's writing submitted to the magazine. For the contest, editors stressed the importance of children's expression of the beauties of nature and daily life situations (Hiraoka, 2011). Although the number of teachers and children interested in such a contest and tsuzurikata itself were relatively small (Namekawa, 1978), many teachers studied these writings as a method of education and the effectiveness of such writings began to spread in the liberal atmosphere of those times.

Following this orientation to pursue children's writings that describe their experiences vividly, tsuzurikata or *seikatsu-tsuzurikata* (*seikatsu* means ordinary life) underwent a boom in the early Showa era (1926–1989), prior to World War II. Given this movement, there was much expansion of tsuzurikata education. Some teachers explored the possibilities of this activity to include other subjects of school education, such as social studies. Other teachers who taught children in economically disadvantaged areas, both in big cities and rural communities, focused on tsuzurikata as a method to allow children to reflect, express, and better understand their lives despite difficulty. For example, Ichitaro Kokubun, who later became one of the leaders of seikatsu-tsuzurikata education, stressed *seikatsu benkyo* (learning in everyday life) as a principle of his seikatsu-tsuzurikata education in 1935 (Funabashi, 1996).

Teachers' devotion to tsuzurikata was widely known in this period and it had an effect on Japanese society. For example, a fourth-grade child's writings about her daily life in economic difficulty, edited by her teachers (Toyoda 1937/1995), became a best seller, and the stories in the book were staged by a professional theatrical company and then cinematized in 1938 (Narita 2001). As the stories by Toyoda were also popular after World War II, children's writings about their lives were widely accepted with sympathy.

On the other hand, the act of writing about the difficulty of daily life and focusing on conflicts in society can be ideologically sensitive. There was even a time in history (1940–1944) when teachers who instructed children to write about their daily lives were arrested and detained. Although the exact number of the teachers arrested in these 5 years is unclear, many were falsely charged and more than ten teachers died due to this incarceration (Namekawa, 1983). This happened in relation to the wider crackdown on political activities of teachers with socialist leanings, and it suggests that making children more aware of their lives through writing was considered a problem by the government during World War II. In wartime, children's writing concentrated on letters for soldiers or celebrating victories (Namekawa, 1983).

Although the pressures of wartime brought about a drastic reduction of tsuzurikata education, teachers restarted it during reconstruction efforts after the war. Teachers and researchers formed societies that offered regular meetings for sharing and discussing children's writings. The number of teachers active in such societies is lower nowadays, but regular writing of nikki stories is still practiced in many classrooms at Japanese elementary schools. These facts represent the uniqueness of these activities in the history of education in Japan, and the teachers' belief in the effectiveness and potential of children writing their experiences.

Children's Writings and Our Understanding of Children's Selves

As mentioned in the previous section, children's writing (or telling) of their experiences was considered to have a relationship with their *selves* from the very early period of modern school education in Japan. We can find many discussions by schoolteachers who worked hard on tsuzurikata or seikatsu-tsuzurikata that referred to the jiko (self) of children as a vital element in their writings, and these discussions were also considered by researchers of education in Japan. For example, Iida (2013) discusses how leading figures in seikatsu-tsuzurikata education in the Taisho and early Showa era debated the understanding of the self in children's writings. Although the nature of the self supposed by these debates varied, many teachers considered children's selves the origin of the unique perspective that enabled their writings. As Iida (2013) also pointed out, the focus on the self in children's writings had an effect, even if indirectly, on the basic policies of *Nihon sakubun no kai,* a major society of teachers and researchers engaged in sakubun education after World War II.

Researchers of the history of education in Japan also interpret these educational practices in relation to the clarification of the self in meaning construction. In the discussion concerning the educational activities by Ichitaro Kokubun, Funabashi (1996) describes Kokubun's orientation toward tsuzurikata as "Every child constructed meaning concerning the actuality, "*I live,*" that is unique to him/her, in relation to trivial events, interactions with others or objects, and troubles" (p. 93, translation by author). Funabashi also suggests that Kokubun's activities enabled the approval of children's meaning construction (i.e., their writings) to support and facilitate their lives in struggling agricultural communities, even if their expressions were sometimes naïve or vulgar.

These frameworks that emphasized children's selves in relation to their writings about their experiences do not elaborate how we can find the self in concrete terms, but instead share a fundamental perspective with my discussion developed in former chapters. Specifically, they emphasized the need for teachers to *find out* children's unique perspectives or personalities that appear in their active writings about their environments and meaning constructions. In other words, the self is considered to be what emerges during the process of children's meaning construction as I discussed in the former chapters, *not* the static representation *inside themselves.*

In addition, children's writings about their experiences are based on the children's everyday transitions between home and school, just as was the mother-child conversation I analyzed. Children clarify what they have experienced at home through the work required by teachers in the institutional environment, and this can be considered the opposite of what occurs in the conversation about children's experiences at yochien or hoikuen. Although the process and the media of meaning construction are different from conversations, this backdrop of children's writings suggests the resemblance in the occurrence of meaning construction in children's lives, as I further elaborate in Chap. 6.

The resemblance of mother-child conversation and children's writings is also evidenced in the difficulty of applying existing methods of psychology to them. As early as 1935, elementary school teachers and researchers explored the possibility of analyzing children's writings from psychological perspectives in relation to their personality, and several presentations concerning tsuzurikata were made at annual conference meetings of the Japanese Psychological Society (Namekawa, 1978).[3] However, psychological inquiries into children's writings in relation to children's development in society did not develop afterwards except for a few explorative studies. Among these rare studies, Moriya, Mori, Hirasaki, and Sakanoe (1972) analyzed stories by 11 children with longitudinally collected data and showed developmental changes in how children describe themselves (e.g., from descriptions of observable characteristics to their own internal status) based on the categorization of writings. However, the absence of research after Moriya, Mori, Hirasaki, and Sakanoe (1972) indicates the difficulty of understanding children's selves from their writings by objective categorization of fragmented pieces of these, just as with the analysis of natural conversation.

From this affinity between children's writings and their selves and the difficulty of applying existing frameworks of psychology to the clarification of the self through writing, I attempt an application of the theoretical framework elaborated in Chap. 4 to the personal stories children write as their work assigned by teachers. Through this analysis, I show the emergence of children's presentational selves in meaning construction based on the written language, which requires different types of dialogical relationships with others.

Approaching Children's Personal Stories in Nikki

To discuss the emergence of children's selves in the meaning construction, here I develop my discussion from the examples of children's writings analyzed in two papers (Komatsu & Konno, 2014; Yamamoto & Komatsu, 2016). In these studies, we collected and analyzed children's writings by copying the notebooks they used. In concrete terms, Komatsu and Konno (2014) discussed the application of the framework of the presentational self using 12 stories from nikki by four children.

---

[3] In the 1930s, researchers of psychology in Japan began to attempt explorations of children's minds through their expressions. Although there was no study of children's writings published in journals of psychology in that time, we can find some published papers concerning children's drawings. For example, Hatano (1932) explored children's experiences of their dreams during sleep through their drawings.

They were extracted from 632 stories written by 26 children in a third-grade class at an elementary school located in the greater Osaka area. The exploration by Yamamoto and Komatsu (2016) compared 14 stories written by three children in the fourth grade at an elementary school located in central Osaka. Each of these three children wrote around 180 such stories in a single academic year (Yamamoto & Komatsu, 2016). All of these stories were used for studies with the consent of parents.

As described in the previous section, the way that children engage in nikki writing varies depending on each teacher's preference. In the examples of Komatsu and Konno (2014), writing personal stories was not obligatory for children. However, most children wrote a story and brought their nikki notebook to the teacher once a week, according to the schedule the teacher set for inspection and response. Conversely, writing a story was an everyday activity for the children appearing in Yamamoto and Komatsu (2016), and they were able to write either at their home or at school. In both classes, teachers added their comments to what children had written, including the teachers' impressions of the children's experiences and some advice for the children.

The number of stories appearing in these two studies is small and the ways that children wrote and teachers responded vary in their details. However, their analyses showed the resembling characteristics in children' writings. In the following section, I will first discuss the basic style of meaning construction that appears frequently in children's writings, using the theoretical framework of the presentational self. Second, I will inquire into further clarification of the self as observed in these writings in relation to dialogical dynamics and the role of others in these processes.

A Fundamental Process of Meaning Construction in Nikki Writing: Describing Events in Time

When we read Japanese children's writings translated into English, we must be aware of differences between the languages reading explicitness of the subject. Specifically, pronouns such as "I," "my," "we," and "our" have been added to the English translations of many sentences shown in the excerpts below, as already indicated in the conversation transcripts. Omitting these pronouns is very ordinary and natural in Japanese language,[4] as described by Hinds (1986), especially in the informal interactions that I analyze in this book. Although this linguistic characteristic bears some relation to how we find the self in meaning construction, the

---

[4] For example, the grammatically correct sentence in Japanese *kyou concert ni itta* can be translated as "I went to a concert today." However, the original does not include any words directly corresponding to "I" or "a" in the translation. In a similar way, *kyou otouto ga concert ni itta* can be translated as "My brother went to a concert today," but again, the expression in Japanese does not include any words for "my" or "a."

framework of the presentational self lets us focus on the *process* of writing, refusing a simple inter-cultural comparison.

Concerning this question, both Komatsu and Konno (2014) and Yamamoto and Komatsu (2016) pointed out children's strong tendency to write their experiences in enumerative style and to follow the flow of time. Excerpts 5.1 and 5.2 are examples typical of the nikki writing of children in the third or fourth grade. Although the topics vary, the children listed what happened and the descriptions follow a time series. Enumerations also appear here: the child who wrote Excerpt 5.1 included what she ate in the first half of the episode, and Excerpt 5.2 begins with the enumeration of tasks that the child performed.

Excerpt 5.1 (From nikki of child A, third grade, June 28) (Komatsu & Konno, 2014, p. 331, Table 4)
Title: A whole day in Shopping mall
Today, [we] visited an Italian restaurant with a buffet at the mall. [The dishes] were very delicious. First, [I] ate some spaghetti and a hamburger steak. Next, [I] ate spaghetti and more hamburger and then roast chicken too. For dessert, [I] ate a pudding, about 10 cream puffs, and then more pudding. [They] were awesome. And then, after some shopping with mom, [we] went to the bookstore. [We] read books for a long time there. And [we] watched a movie. [It] was really fun. Mom, my sister, and I enjoyed it. At the end, they got married and [the woman] got pregnant. Because there were sudden interruptions in the sound twice, [they] gave [us] free tickets for some juice [as compensation for the accident]. [We] did some other shopping and returned home. Because [it] was raining when [we] went home, dad came [to help us]. [It] was a very long day today.

Excerpt 5.2 (From nikki of child B, fourth grade, March 9) (Yamamoto & Komatsu, 2016, p. 80, Table 2)
Yesterday, [I] went to [my] lessons [at a *juku*, or private tutoring school in Japan]. Sheets [I did] were two sheets of [doing] written calculation of decimals and four sheets of English. [I] made one or two mistakes in the sheets concerning decimals and calculating decimals. [I] got "100 [perfect score], very good" in all four sheets of English. When [I] came home, [I] finished the homework from school. After that, [I] went to [another] *juku*. [I] did mathematics because [it] was Thursday. First, [we] did a confirmation test. [I] got 16 points in common questions and 0 point in "S-questions." The task in the lesson was thinking of a number to fit the blank space. [It] was difficult. But [it] became little easier because [our] teacher gave [us] some instruction how [to do it]. [I] returned home at six forty-five when *juku* was over.

Notes: Excerpts appearing in this chapter were originally shown in Komatsu and Konno (2014) and Yamamoto and Komatsu (2016), and were translated from Japanese by the author. Small revisions were made from the original. All the names are pseudonyms. Words in brackets show contextual and additional information included for clarification. Omitted subjects and other pronouns are also shown with brackets. The academic year in Japan begins in April and ends in March.

This characteristic is widely observable and consistent with Japan's national education guidelines. For example, this style of writing is already pointed out in

Moriya et al. (1972). National guidelines for education also stipulate that children should learn to describe their experiences sequentially when they are in the first grade and second grade at elementary school. For the third grade and fourth grade, the national guidelines recommend teaching children how to focus on what they intend to write and express, including planning what to write in each paragraph in advance. These academic and institutional guidelines imply that such expressions are based on the repertoire of expressions that children in third grade and fourth grade are capable of handling (Komatsu & Konno, 2014).

This fundamental characteristic is a way of externalizing from the stream of consciousness by selective reduction in writing (Zittoun & Gillespie, 2012): that is, microgenesis of meaning. In other words, the writings by children are objective traces of meaning construction that were made from their unique perspectives that reflect the existence of their selves. To elaborate this process further, in the next section I turn to the semiotic processes and the dialogical structure at work in writing.

The Self in the Construction of Ordered Configurations of Events

As I pointed out in Chap. 3, enumeration based on a variety of frames (e.g., enumeration of friends in relation to their roles in a theater performance) serves to clarify children's selves as Gestalt quality. Through the meaning construction, it works to construct a configuration in which a child is positioned.[5] If I apply this framework to the meaning construction in the excerpts above, the configuration of the events may work to make the presentational self emerge.

To elaborate the process of meaning construction in writing and inquire into the presentational self within this, I attempt a description of the underlined passages of Excerpt 1 using the framework of meanacting introduced in Chap. 3. Although some details have been omitted, this enumerative description in time series can be illustrated as Fig. 5.3. Firstly, it begins with a meaning field concerning what the child ate at the restaurant. Mentioning several dishes (**A**) accompanies the potential field of development (**non-A**) that might possibly include other dishes, who was there, what they talked about, and so forth. From these possibilities, the child includes another dish (roast chicken) in the next sentence that can be described as **a'** in its connection with **A**. After introducing the dessert she ate (**B**), it is taken over by a new field concerning shopping (**C**) that developed in **non-B**.

In this process, construction of these fields proceeds in a more orderly fashion and includes more information when compared to the meanacting in the conversa-

---

[5] Although Excerpts 5.1 and 5.2 do not include enumeration of others, children often make lists of others, especially their friends, at the beginning of their stories (see Excerpts 5.6 and 5.8 for examples).

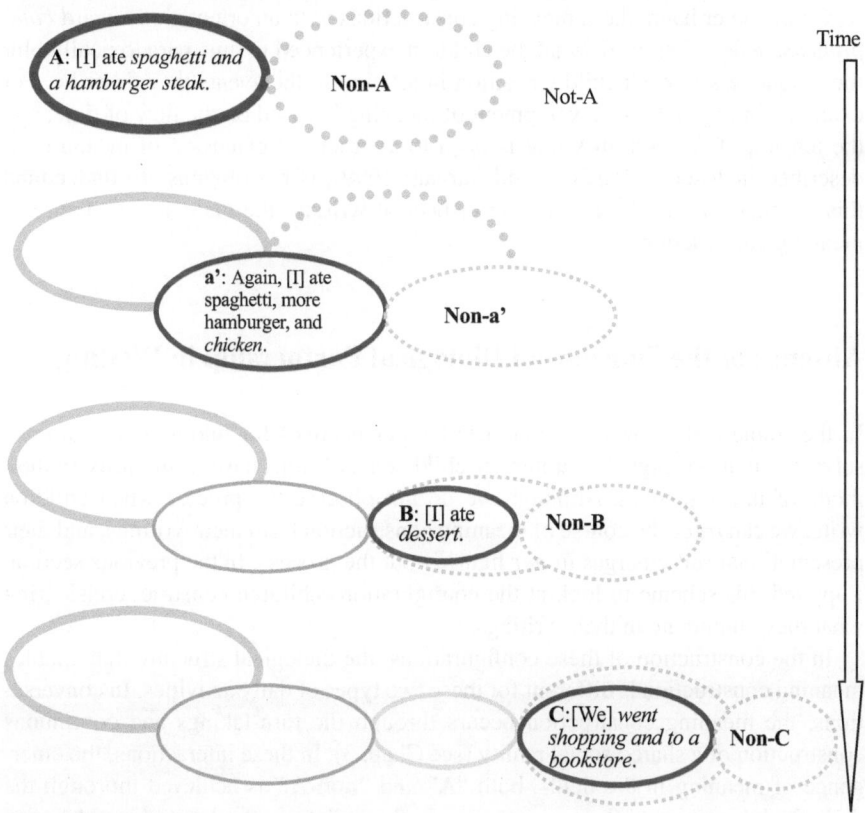

Fig. 5.3 Meaning complexes constituted in the writing of Excerpt 5.1

tion of a 5 year-old child (see Fig. 3.2 for example). In other words, what will be mentioned next in the writing—that is, how the field of possible meaning (e.g., **non-A**) works in the process—is greatly based on the perspective on *what was there* or *what happened next* (Komatsu & Konno, 2014).

The use of these frames still shows the existence of children's unique perspectives in finding what to write. For example, the description of what a girl ate in a restaurant clarifies her interest in foods, in comparison with the title of the books in the bookstore, and the child describing his scores (Excerpt 5.2) clarifies the priority of his achievements in comparison to listing who was there. Thus, following the definition, we can find the presentational selves of the children in the configurations they construct in relation to the objects or events they describe, even when the subject "I" is not explicitly mentioned. Through the description of what dishes the girl ate at the restaurant or what scores the boy achieved at *juku* (private tutoring school), we can find their positioning of themselves in relation to the commercial products they enjoy or the value of studying they must perform.

On the other hand, these meaning constructions with an orientation toward *comprehensive* descriptions of what the children experienced in time paradoxically blur the uniqueness of each child's position in relation to the events they describe. For example, in Fig. 5.3, the development of meaning is based on the flow of time, and the tension of **A** <> **non-A** that is open to a variety of extension of meaning, as described in Josephs, Valsiner, and Surgan (1999), is not obvious. To understand this inertness, I will discuss another aspect of writing: the dialogical structure of meaning construction.

Absence of the Substantial Dialogical Partnership in Writing

In the framework shown in Table 4.1, the perspectives for finding out children's selves in their writings and in mother-child conversations have a similarity in their mode of understanding. Although we do not observe the process when children write, we can *trace* the course of meaning construction from their writings, and their presentational self emerges in *our* figuring out the process. In the previous section, I applied this scheme to look at the configurations children construct considering what they enumerate in their writings.

In the construction of these configurations, the dialogical structure that enables meaning construction is different for these two types of daily activities. In conversations, the meaning construction occurs through the turn-takings and continuous construction of a shared social reality (see Chap. 3). In these interactions, the emergence of meaning in the fields, both "A" and "**non-A**," is achieved thorough the dialogical dynamics of the conversation. In these dialogical relationships, the partner in the conversation works literally as the *other* that introduces the differentiation of meaning.

In this dialogical relationship, participants share the topics to develop in the interaction, but often relate differently to the possible field of meaning construction. For example, the name of a girl whom a child meets every day at hoikuen may bring up for the child the games they played together that day. However, for the child's mother, the same name may work to remind her of the lovely clothes the girl was wearing when she last saw her. Thus, from the perspective of the child, her mother can introduce new meaning in relation to what she mentioned in conversation. Although such an actualization of new meaning may not always be smooth, conversational interaction has the potential to activate the dynamics.

In contrast, writing stories is something children do by themselves. The results of a survey by Yamamoto and Komatsu (2016) in which 218 fourth grade children participated showed that over half of the children either never or very rarely showed their nikki notebooks to family members. This suggests it is rare for children in the third or fourth grade to write their experiences through interactions with others: that is, with help from their parents. Thus, I illustrate how children accomplish this work

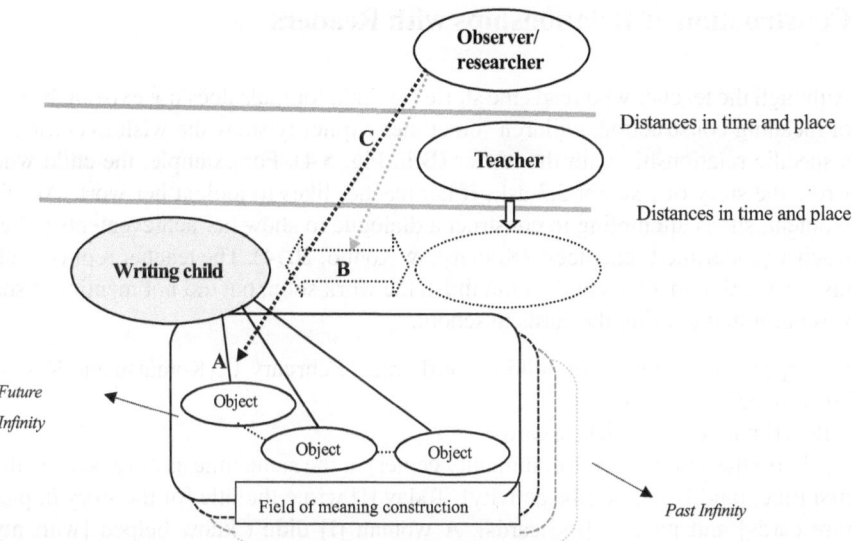

Fig. 5.4 The framework of children's writings about their experiences

and how we find their selves by modifying the basic framework of the presentational self (Fig. 4.2) as Fig. 5.4.

As I discussed in the foregoing sections, the configuration of a child and what he or she describes in stories (e.g., dishes at a restaurant, scores in tasks at juku), which is designated by **A** in Fig. 5.4, can be understood as similar to what we observed in the configuration of self and others constructed in mother-child conversations. In some sense, children's writings show clearer order by clarifying what existed in the site of their experiences precisely. However, the inter-individual relationship for meaning construction is qualitatively different from that of conversations. The dialogical dynamics that exist in conversation (**B** in Fig. 5.4) do not work at the inter-individual level and children must construct it within themselves—that is, they write their experiences *considering* that their teacher will read it afterwards. This type of dialogical relationship is characteristic of the writing upon which I will elaborate in the following discussion.

This absence of substantial dialogical dynamics is also related to the field of meaning construction. As children use written language, it exists objectively in front of them and the result of meaning construction is also observable for the children. However, this objective nature and the imaginary dialogue with teachers restrict the possibility of extending meaning construction further to, for example, past infinities or future infinities. In other words, it is more difficult to leap into other topics that just came up in their thinking, without any clear connection to what they have already written. Within this meaning construction in isolation, children's frequent use of enumeration and focus on the flow of the time, which are very powerful devices of meaning construction, are rational.

Construction of Relationships with Readers

Although the teacher who reads the stories in nikki journals does not exist in the site of meaning construction, children sometimes explicitly show the wish to construct a specific relationship with the reader (**B** in Fig. 5.4). For example, the child who wrote the story of Excerpt 5.3 asks if her teacher likes to look at her work. At this moment, she is attempting to construct a dialogue to show her achievements to her teacher (underlined sentences) (Komatsu & Konno, 2014). The teacher replied with his expectation that the child would finish the work soon, but did not mention if she was permitted to bring the cards to school.

Excerpt 5.3 (From nikki of child C, third grade, February 1) (Komatsu and Konno 2014, p. 332, Table 5)
Title: [I] painted (my picture cards)
[I] Go [to the activity in the community center] at the same time as always, even the first time, [and I] join in [the activity]. Today [I] wrote the title [of the story in picture cards] and painted [the cards]. A woman [I] didn't know helped [with my work]. [We] did a lot of work and were happy. [I] thought [I] would do the rest [of the work] at [my] home. [My] mom said "[You] will get further [with your work] if [you] did [it] at home." Mami [the child's name] asked another person who worked as a coach, "Can [I] paint [them] at [my] home?" And [she] said "Yes." After [I] came back [home, I] played [Nintendo] DS. [I] played two [video game] cassettes. [We] will have an exhibition and performance of storytelling with picture cards [that we made]. [I] will show you [the cards] in school after [they are] completed. [Would you] like to see [them]? [I] will bring [them] if [you] want. What would [you] like? [Today] was a very fun and happy day.

Even if not expressed explicitly, as in this example, description of one's achievements can serve as an attempt to construct a dialogue that brings children some desirable response (e.g., praise from their teacher). Yamamoto and Komatsu (2016) interpret the repeated appearance of stories very similar to Excerpt 5.2 (e.g., description of tasks and scores) in the nikki of child B as the presentation of himself as someone who steadily completes the tasks at the juku he attends.

Such a construction of quasi-dialogical relationship with the teacher is not limited to showing off achievements that could possibly lead to a teacher's interest, approval, or praise. Yamamoto and Komatsu (2016) describe a child who repeatedly claims that her life does not contain remarkable events to write about; one example is given in Excerpt 5.4. As her story is very short and she clearly declares there was nothing special (underlined sentences), this writing can be interpreted as her moderate objection to the obligatory task of writing. Although not in reply to this writing task, her teacher did encourage her to write her feelings or thoughts (Yamamoto & Komatsu, 2016). However, dynamics of positioning like we found in the mother-child conversation hardly ever occur in institutional settings, even if teachers emphasize that children can write their experiences freely.

Excerpt 5.4 (From nikki of child D, fourth grade, September 28) (Yamamoto & Komatsu, 2016, p. 82, Table 3)
I did nothing special yesterday. [I] forgot what [I] ate yesterday. [I] played tag with [my] friends during breaks at school. [I] hadn't [played tag] for quite a while. [I] sweated a lot. As [it] will get colder soon, [we] play outside a lot. [Playing tag] was really fun because [we] hadn't done it for a long time.

Different Types of Otherness in the Process of Writing

The discussion concerning the dialogical structure in children's nikki writings also suggests how otherness works in meaning construction. In the process of writing, what children wrote in their notebooks are the externalized traces of their meaning construction. Similar to the process I described in Fig. 4.4, extended from the idea of Mead (1934), they construct an immediate feedback loop to clarify "me" as the consequence of the acting "I." This also suggests that children's writings bring about not only the presentational self for observers (readers), but also the sense of self for children themselves, as Mead (1934) discussed: "(…) when taking the attitude of the other becomes an essential part in his behavior- then the individual appears in his own experience as a self" (p. 195).

Given this thinking, the dialogical interaction in Fig. 5.4 is elaborated as Fig. 5.5. The emergence of the presentational self is observable in the dialogical loops

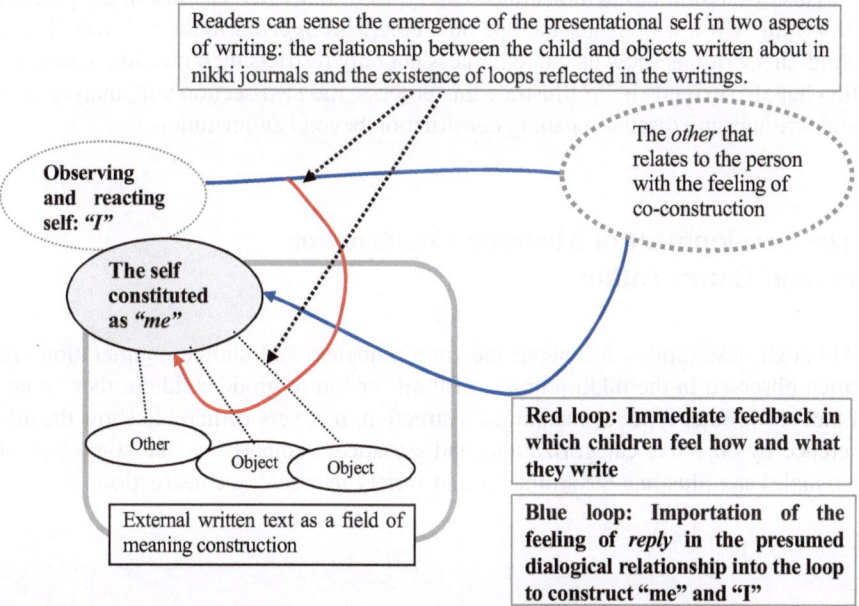

Fig. 5.5 Self-perception in the act of writing and the emergence of the presentational self

children construct and the result of meaning construction that we observers find in their writings. By describing what happened or what was there, the child is constantly relating to his or her environments. As the examples of Excerpts 5.3 and 5.4 describe, this process is sustained by the loops children rely on when they construct the field of meaning construction.

In this process, externalized writings work powerfully with *otherness*: "… the existence of something on its own account, autonomously, independently of the I's initiative, volition, consciousness, and recognition" (Petrilli, 2013, p. 10). As Petrilli (2013) has discussed in her thinking concerning the self and the sign, this otherness does not necessarily inhabit a person, but is rather "a synonym for 'materiality'" (p. 10). However, otherness working here is not limited to the materiality of what children wrote. As I described above, children presume readers or teachers who exist beyond their writings. Although nikki writing is, by consensus of pupils and teachers, non-evaluative in comparison with other tasks in school education, teachers strongly represent the value of achievements or efforts for children. In the process of writing, teachers serve as assumed others for the constitution of "me" in this process.

As I discussed in the previous section, otherness is not limited to what emerges through active and substantial interactions with others, but rather what works as a restriction upon children's actions toward their environments. Writing words in the notebook and following grammatical rules to construct a readable story leads the meaning construction along some restricted paths, and the teacher as an internalized other potentially requires stories that are worth reporting, as a child clarifies in her complaint (Excerpt 5.4).

This discussion has demonstrated two types of otherness at work in the process of writing, but this does not include how otherness *appears* in the writings. These children's writings show us that otherness not only restricts their meaning construction but also extends it. To illustrate this process, the next section will analyze several writings and discuss meaning construction beyond enumeration.

The Development of Meaning Construction beyond Enumeration

Although descriptions following the time sequence and simple enumeration are often observed in the nikki journals of third- or fourth-grade children, they sometimes show other types of meaning construction. It is very difficult to show the difference by objective categorizations and statistical comparisons, but some typical examples can illustrate the similarity and variety in meaning construction.

Excerpt 5.5 (From nikki of child A, third grade, February 25) (Komatsu & Konno, 2014, p. 331, Table 4)

Title: Mom's milk jelly.

Today, three [of my] sister's friends came over [to my house]. [We] all ate snacks. The sweets everyone [the friends] brought us, mini-donuts, potato chips, and choco- late, and juice and milk jelly that [my] mom made yesterday. I love mom's milk jelly a lot. [It] is really delicious. Yamashita [a friend]'s mom gave [us] the recipe for the jelly when I was at kindergarten. [My] mom promised [me] to show [me] how to make it when I get older. [I'm] looking forward to it.

Excerpt 5.5 was written by the child who wrote the story in Excerpt 5.1, and it is very short in comparison with the previous story. After introducing an event, she enumerates what they ate at her house. This is similar to the meaning construction in Excerpt 5.1 also described in Fig. 5.3, which relies on *what were there*. However, her perspective expands from the "milk jelly" into her personal preference for it and the close interpersonal relationships between her mother, her friend (Yamashita)'s mother, and herself (underlined sentences). This transition in meaning construction also encompasses a shift in time: this short story deals with her experiences of that day, her kindergarten days, and her future relationship with her mother. Thus, the child extends the meaning of an event and in this construction of multiple relation- ships with an object (i.e., milk jelly), her uniqueness in relation to others becomes clearer for the reader. Moreover, though it could be incidental, the subject "I" (ordi- narily implicit in Japanese) is stated repeatedly to show the girl's subjective stand- point in this part of the story (Komatsu & Konno, 2014).

What is observed here resembles the result of a comparison between the episodes of conversation (e.g., Excerpt 1.2 in which Mina and her mother constructed a sim- ple enumeration of Mina and her friends and Excerpt 3.2, which shows a variety of relationships between Mina and one of her friends, who was first included in the enumeration). In other words, children's meaning construction that clarifies their presentational selves is often based on simple enumeration but it occasionally becomes the starting point for further meaning constructions that position the child in a complex, tangled configuration of persons and objects. Further, the comparison of Excerpts 1.5 and 5.5 suggests that in children's writings, great length or volume does not necessarily imply complex development of meaning construction.

The presentational self emerging in the configuration of variety of episodes shows the unique perspective of the child to the observers (Fig. 5.6). That is, the extension of meaning construction in the latter half of Excerpt 5.5 shows the active functioning of the **non-A** field from which a child's unique perspective chooses one possible extension, rather than relying on a single fixed way (Komatsu & Konno, 2014). When the meaning developed from the first description (**A**: I love this milk jelly, with the implicit contrast with **non-A**: Anything that is not this kind of jelly, but has some relationship with the jelly or her mother) to the second (**a'**: It is deli- cious, also contrasted with possible other descriptions that have some relationship

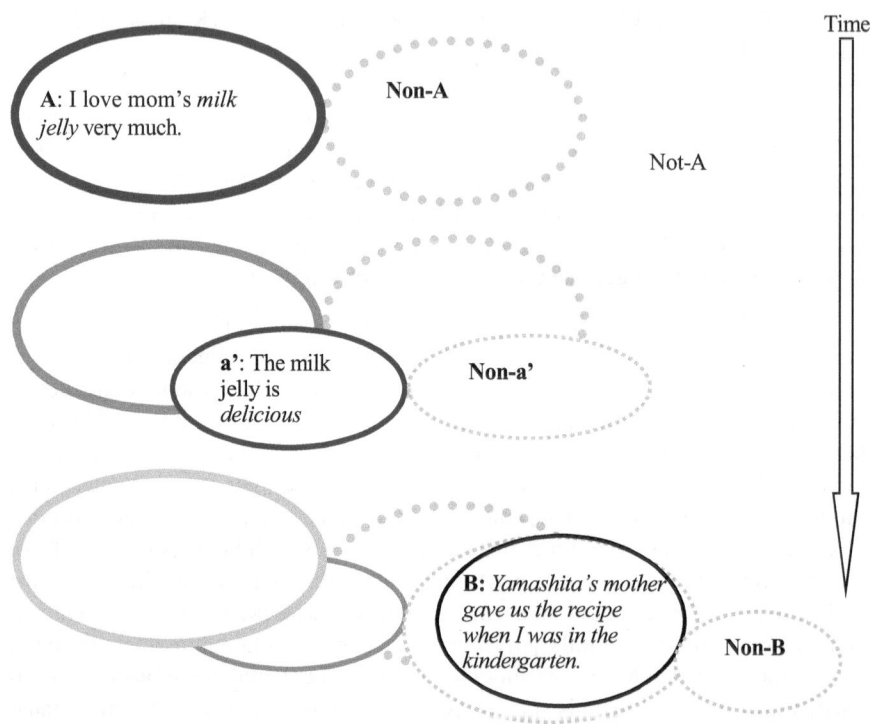

Fig. 5.6 Meaning complexes constituted in the writing of Excerpt 5.5

to the deliciousness of the jelly, **non-a**), the fields **a'** and **non-a'** carry the potential for further development of meaning. As I discussed, what was there (e.g., I also drank some delicious juice) or what happened next (e.g., Then we played a game) are frequent choices from these possibilities. However, the child introduces a totally different development at this point by bringing up an event from the far past (**B**). This leap into the past clarifies the child's own perspective and positions her in a long-lasting relationship with her friend's family. After this, she continues on to describe her relationship with her mother in the future.

The Extension of Meaning Construction into the Details of Experiences

Meaning construction beyond enumerative description is not limited to extensions into the past or future. Komatsu and Konno (2014) also showed the shifting of children's perspectives toward the details of internal or interpersonal interactions as another type of writing that clarifies the unique perspective of children (e.g., Excerpt 5.3). Excerpt 5.6 is another example that includes both interpersonal dialogue and internal utterances, written by the same child who wrote the story of Excerpt 5.4.

Excerpt 5.6 (From nikki of child D, fourth grade, May 11) (Yamamoto & Komatsu, 2016, p. 82, Table 3)

Yesterday, I played with Kana, Rika, and Misa. [We] played at Kana's house. [We] played Jenga. Misa did not play [as she was] reading a book. Partway through, [Misa] said "[I'll] play," [and we] let [her] play, but Misa tried to take a block right from the middle so Rika and I said "Don't take it." [Misa] cried and [I] got annoyed. [I] thought to myself "Ah, [I] don't like little sisters," although Misa is Rika's little sister ... [Misa] was crying until [we] finished Jenga. Rika lost [the game] in the end. Next [we] played the Tamagotchi Game of Life. I came last. Misa stopped crying when [we] played Tamagotchi and [we] enjoyed [it] together. [It] was fun enough.

The story of Excerpt 5.6 begins with enumeration of the children who played together and ends with the description of what the child did in a time sequence. However, the child writing the story focuses on the younger sister of her friend (Misa), describing some conflict with her. Although her description is a simple succession of events and includes many ellipses, it develops from Misa's sudden participation, a short exchange and Misa's emotional outburst, and the child's reaction to it (underlined sentences). She even includes an expression of disapproval of her friend's younger sister, which may not be congruent with the values emphasized at the school. This suggests that this incident was the most impressive to her in the series of events in their playing together, and the detail of interaction and internal reaction clarifies her unique perspective to it (Yamamoto & Komatsu, 2016).

This shift of children's perspective to the details is also observable in the writings of the third-grade children (Excerpts 5.7, 5.8). In the story of Excerpt 5.7, the child initially intended to describe his trip to an aquarium with his family, as the title shows. However, the detailed description of his conversation with his parents is far clearer in the story (underlined sentences), and his experiences in the aquarium are not elaborated (Komatsu & Konno, 2014). If the story is evaluated focusing on his ability to write what he initially intended, it might not be assessed as particularly excellent. However, the sudden shift of his focus onto the fine details of the conversation clarifies his *subjective* experience of anger or surprise.

Excerpt 5.7 (From nikki of child E, third grade, July) (Komatsu & Konno, 2014, p. 329, Table 2)

Title: [We] went to an aquarium.

[We] went to Kaiyu-kan [an aquarium in Osaka]. Dad said "Let's go to an aquarium" because [we were] free. Mom said "Then why don't [we] go to Kaiyu-kan?" [I] played [a video] game during the ride, because [I] felt bored. After [I'd] played [the game] for eleven minutes or so, Dad said "Quit the game" and [I] asked "Why?" [He] said "[We]'ve arrived" but [there was] nothing there. [I] blamed [him], saying "[You're a] liar, [I] can't see [it]," and [my] mom said "[We] take a bus [from here]", and [we] took a bus. [We] arrived [at the aquarium] soon. [We] walked through, looking at the fish. As [we] went down [from the top of the aquarium building] gradually, [I] found a sign saying "Jellyfish." [I] couldn't see [them] because [it] was very crowded. But [I] enjoyed [the aquarium], and [we] went home after eating ice cream.

The story of Excerpt 5.8 basically enumerates the child's actions in a time line. However, at some points, his own viewpoint becomes clearer when he directly describes his reactions to this experience using a dialogical or direct speech style (underlined sentences). Although this is a simple move, the shift clarifies the child's subjective position in relation to specific details of the events (Komatsu and Konno 2014).

Excerpt 5.8 (From the diary of child F, third grade, October 9) (Komatsu & Konno, 2014, p. 330, Table 3)
Today, [I] played with Matsuno. When [I] arrived at Matsuno's, his brother and [his brother's] friend were there. Matsuno's brother's friend said "Let's play Mario Cart," so [we] played it using [wireless] networking. But [I] was the worst at it. [I] wondered "Why?" Next [we] played a balloon battle. Again, [my] score was very bad. After the balloon battle, [(unclear)]. Then [I] played action figures with Matsuno. After playing with figures, [we] practiced soccer really hard. First, [we] did strong kicking. [We] did well. Then [we] had a match. Matsuno did a good kick. I also did a good one. Next, [we] tested [our] best kicks. Matsuno kicked and the ball flew high, but mine didn't. [I] wondered "Why?" It's because [I] kicked [the ball] with [my] hands in [my] pockets. After soccer, [I] played DS at Matsuno's house, then went home. [It] was a veeery enjoyable day.

The examples shown in Excerpts 5.5, 5.6, 5.7, 5.8 illustrate the emergence of the children's unique perspectives in relation to their experiences. The development of meaning only by enumerating what was there or what happened is smooth and offers generalized descriptions that potentially lead to further elaboration. In other words, differentiation of meanings through the child's reactions to others creates his or her uniqueness in relation to what is described.

Introducing Dialogue into the Field of Meaning Construction

The examples of Excerpts 5.6 and 5.7 that describe the detail of interaction the child experienced typically show the clarification of the uniqueness of the child in relation to his or her environments. As I discussed previously, the enumerative description of what was seen or what was done also clarifies the child's position in relation to the listed objects. In contrast to this, the detail of events appearing in these writings fixes the "I" of them that responds to the others' actions.

The process can be described as in Fig. 5.7, by superimposing another dialogical loop indicated by the green lines onto Fig. 5.5. In this process, the description of interaction is performed in the substantial field of meaning construction—i.e., the notebook for writing personal stories—and a child constitutes *Me (in writing)*." The dialogue with the other (e.g., Misa in Excerpt 5.6) reflects *I (in the event)*" of the child that responds to the other's action (e.g., suddenly began to cry) and constitutes *Me (in the event),*" which both become a part of *Me (in writing)*." Thus, inclusion

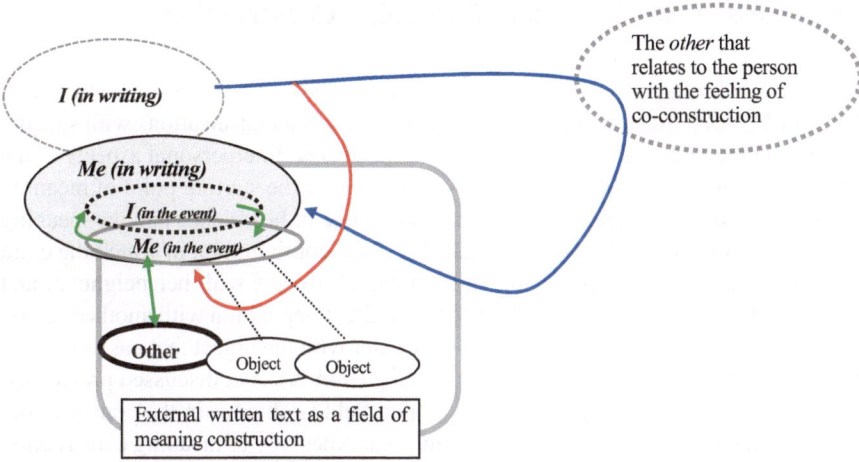

Fig. 5.7 Introduction of dialogical interaction into the field of meaning construction

of dialogue with others in writing is the elaboration of positioning in relation to others, and readers (observers) can find the child's presentational self as more distinct and unique through the clarification of the dialogical loop that the child experienced on site.

At least in the examples above, the emotional reactions of children play an important role. Introducing conversations into writings is sometimes recommended to children by teachers to more vividly express what they have experienced,[6] and it is plausible that children who wrote these stories had previously received such advice. However, the conversations included in Excerpts 5.6 and 5.7 are probably *not* the results of carefully planned composition intended to maximize the impact of each story, considering the numerous ellipses in Excerpt 5.6 or the gap between the title and the story in Excerpt 5.7. These are candid expressions of what was most impressive, in somewhat negative ways, of the series of events each child experienced. Children's selves become clearer for both children and readers through this opposition. This observation is consistent with the discussion in a previous inquiry into children's writings (Moriya et al. 1972), which insisted that children's self-consciousness emerges in their critical recognition of others who interrupt their intentional acts or claims. This is not limited to interpersonal opposition, but also appears in the conflicts that children experience as the result of their acts. The direct description of the child's internal utterance in Excerpt 5.8 is not the type featuring inter-individual interaction, but another type of clarification of self in children's dialogical interaction with their environments.

---

[6]These instructions for including conversation into writing already appeared in a book about Japanese language education published before World War II (Namekawa, 1983).

Otherness as the Promoter of Meaning Construction

In contrast with the discussion of the previous section, the meaning construction in Excerpt 5.5, also illustrated in Fig. 5.6, does not rely on conversations with specific others and the child describes no conflict in the events. Interpersonal aspects of the self are still at work in this process, however, because the starting point of meaning construction (the milk jelly) is closely related to one of her friends and the meaning that develops from it is highly relational. Thus, the configuration in which the child is positioned includes long-lasting and emotional aspects with her neighbors and her mother. In this process, otherness is not in direct opposition with another person but rather what is at work in the child's encounter with the object that has the potential to extend the possible field of new meaning (**non-A**). As I discussed previously, the extension of meaning from this semi-open field is obvious in the conversation. In contrast, what is appearing in this writing is another way of meaning construction from an *inanimate* partner in the dialogue. In other words, the jelly works as a catalyst for constructing a new meaning.

To sum up, my discussion here has suggested several types of otherness functioning in the process of writing, in addition to the objectivity of written words and the presumption of the reader (teacher) behind these texts. In the process of meaning construction, which is primarily constructed through several stereotypical means, children sometimes focus on the details of their interactions with others that caused them to react emotionally. As relationships with others often include oppositions or conflicts, they work here with a strong sense of otherness that is independent from I's "initiative" or "volition."

Otherness working in writings is not limited to such dialogues or interactions with other person. In the examples I cited, children extended meanings from the results of their acts or the objects they encountered. As I will discuss in Chap. 6, the occurrence of such meaning construction is not predictable and it is difficult to describe a clear developmental trajectory at the ontogenetic level. However, in comparison with natural conversation, children's repeated writings of their experiences may help them perform a variety of meaning construction on the basis of the diverse otherness they can find in their environments.

Conclusion: The Presentational Self from Multiple Dialogues in Writings

The discussion in this chapter showed the applicability of the presentational self into the writings of children. In common with what was found in the recordings of mother-child conversations, children's writings construct configurations of what they recognized in the environments in which they are positioned. In the analysis of conversation, I concentrated on the appearance of others as that which achieves contrast with the child. As an extension of this discussion, I explored the emergence of presentational selves in relation to what is described (e.g., dishes in a restaurant, scores in an academic task) that reflects their perspective on their environments.

Similarly to the emergence of the presentational self through conversation, it is what we find in the process of microgenesis that is figured out as the differentiation of the field of meaning with the dialectic tension of $A <> $ **non-A**. However, the important difference between conversations and written stories lies in the role of other(s) at work in the process. In contrast with dynamic and temporary processes of mother-child conversations, in which the partner in conversation serves as a powerful agent for extending meaning, children must engage in writing by themselves. In this non-interactive way of meaning construction, children's writings often rely on simple methods of extension, such as "what was there" and "what happened next."

In relation to this non-existence of the partner in meaning construction, I showed several types of otherness at work in this process, drawing examples from children's writings. First, writing constructs the substantial, external traces of the work: that is, written sentences which both guide *and* restrict further extension of meaning. At the same time, the potential reader of the story, i.e., the teacher, functions internally as the assumed other who will give children responses to their writings. Thus, the fundamental structure involves two types of otherness that clarify the "me" for children themselves. Second, a dialogical structure also sometimes appears in the description of events and clarifies the self that responds to otherness. This often takes the form of direct descriptions of interaction or conversation with another person, but inanimate objects also carry the potential to promote meaning construction.

Considering these processes that clarify children's selves both for themselves and readers, schoolteachers' emphases on the development of the self in their practice of tsuzurikata or seikatsu-tsuzurikata, which appeared repeatedly in Japan's history, are quite apposite. From the discussion here, many teachers' intention to promote children's development despite economic and social difficulties using seikatsu-tsuzurikata was their attempt to construct "I" and "me" for children who react to a range of uncomfortable experiences in their lives. Although children's writings do not immediately bring about change in their thinking, teachers were aware of the occasional emergence of clear self in the repetition of writings.

In contrast with these patient approaches to children's selves in history, contemporary academics have come to expect the exact conditions in which elaborated writing appears. However, it is difficult to predict or describe when and how children will write stories like those cited in my discussion. For example, the writings of the child who wrote the stories from Excerpts 5.1 and 5.5 do not show any clear trends in an academic year. Children's stories reflect a variety of elements in their lives, and a child's self becomes clearer, whimsically, in the fluctuations of repeated writings, similar to the emergence of self in daily conversations. To understand the incidental nature of the processes discussed here, I will next elaborate the structure of our lives and children's lives that requires meaning constructions and emergence of selves.

Chapter 6
Reunion with Others: Foundations of the Presentational Self in Daily Lives

In this chapter, I further explore the fundamental dynamics that bring about the emergence of children's presentational selves. These were discussed in the foregoing chapters on the basis of children's meaning construction in two types of activity: mother-child conversations and children's writing of personal stories. These all happened in *natural* settings, and in relation to the methods of data collection, I discussed the methodological and epistemological differences between many studies in developmental psychology concerning children's selves (e.g., self-understanding, self-esteem) and the framework of the presentational self. The self is now what emerges to be observed in the meaning construction required in the ordinary lives of children, not a reflection of stable entities that children internally maintain.

To pursue the nature of the framework under discussion, we must elaborate the understanding of *how children's presentational selves distinctly emerge* in their lives. For example, rich meaning construction with a detailed figure of a child's self occurs only rarely and whimsically in recurring conversation. So why do children only *occasionally* engage in the meaning construction that makes their selves more differentiated? This is also a question that concerns the relationship between the episodic and the general natures of our minds. Although our minds work within the episodic contexts we pass through every day, how can we understand this in relation to the *general* aspects of our minds that are constantly at work?[1]

To answer this question, I first focus on the potential of mundane environments and the role of *reunion* that exists in children's (and more generally, our own) lives. Our recurring meetings with other people or objects in our daily lives can be a starting point for meaning construction. What becomes crucial in this movement are several dialectic tensions that exist at the foundation of these reunions. The dialectic tensions are "visible <> invisible" and "same <> non-same", and they promote meaning construction concerning children in the past, present, and future.

---

[1] The relationship between the episodic and the general here is comparable with the distinction between episodic memory and semantic memory (Tulving 1972). They are considered different systems, but they overlap in some aspects and construct the system as a whole.

© The Author(s) 2019
K. Komatsu, *Meaning-Making for Living*, SpringerBriefs in Psychology,
https://doi.org/10.1007/978-3-030-19926-5_6

Why Do Children (and We) *Occasionally* Go Into and Develop Meaning Construction?

Although it sounds very ordinary for us, since we do not carefully examine our conversations every day, episodes of conversation that clarify children's presentational selves, as do the excerpts in Chap. 3, do not appear frequently in natural settings. For example, as shown in Chap. 3, over 34 h of recorded conversation between Mina and her mother included only 50 episodes that referred to Mina and her friends at hoikuen. Children's writings as discussed in Chap. 5 were also non-stable: that is, uncovering consistent ontogenetic changes in their meaning construction from the stories written in a single academic year proves difficult. They would often write very simple stories in the days after producing a story including a variety of meaning constructions (for example, their focus on the details of interaction and their own internal dialogue).

The question of this instability of repeated meaning construction has not been discussed seriously in studies of psychology that consider variations or fluctuations of our everyday conduct as measurement errors to be ignored. In the studies of developmental psychology concerning mother-child conversation, researchers *asked* children and their parents in specially prepared settings to talk about past experiences, rather than waiting for natural occurrence of conversation (Chap. 4). However, if we rely on the framework of Fig. 2.1, we must consider the entirety of the constructed interactions in which children are involved, and elaborate the process. In other words, we must understand not only the process of our dialogue but also what leads it.

This does not mean that existing studies failed to consider the way children participate in the work of meaning construction. In particular, studies involving mother-child conversations have explained that parents who take part in conversations play an important role in this process. As we saw when analyzing the excerpts, an episode of conversation often starts with the mother's (or another adult's) questioning about what a child has experienced. Many studies emphasized the parents' role in conversation, focusing on individual differences of their *elaboration:* i.e., frequent use of open questions and providing details of the children's experiences during the conversation (Fivush, Haden, & Reese, 2006). In addition, as briefly introduced in Chap. 3, the importance of facilitating the conversation is also recognized by the mothers themselves (e.g., for gathering information concerning their children's behaviors) (Komatsu, 2000, 2013). However, these discussions do not fully explain *why mothers like to ask questions*, as they lack the description of fundamental dynamics that bring about the conversation.

For children's writings about their experiences, many schoolteachers kept records of how they had read and interpreted each child's stories. Among these records, some were considered fine educational practices and became well known. However, for this reason, they do not necessarily explain the whimsical nature of the writings. Teachers described the struggles in life or the beauty of innocence observed in children's stories through their educational efforts. However, these particular stories were essentially picked up from among vast numbers of stories as fine and moving examples, and as such, they are not necessarily applicable to the daily practices described in Chap. 5. Further, as already discussed in Chap. 5, studies of developmental psychology and educational psychology failed to develop detailed analyses of these writings in relation to children's development in society.

Thus, to understand these processes further, we need to move from a psychological concept of *style* or *motivation* for conversation and the background of children's writings that includes personal problems (e.g., economic difficulties mentioned in tsuzurikata before WWII) to the more abstract, general dynamics in our lives that promote children's meaning construction. In this inquiry, I examine our lives at two levels of abstraction—one in the structure observable within the practices of our lives, and another at a more abstract level of the dialectic dynamics. They work in close relationship with each other to promote meaning construction that leads to the emergence of the presentational self.

The Potential of Mundane Settings for Meaning Construction

For this inquiry, first we must understand the potential of children's mundane environments to clarify who they are. In the school setting, children encounter multiple meaning systems they use to position themselves. There are, for example, children's shoe shelves and desks standardized in both size and design (Fig. 6.1):

Fig. 6.1 A classroom in a Japanese elementary school (first grade) (Komatsu, 2015, p. 288, Figure 17.1)
Note: The pictures were taken and used with permission

objects that don't exist in their home. These are almost entirely fixed, non-changing environments and serve as a stable order in which children can position themselves. Their institutionalized meanings are clear (e.g., "*I* have *my* shoe box in the second tier, because the nameplates of the boxes are in alphabetical order and *my* name begins with T"). Thus, the familiarity of children's mundane environments serves to stabilize who they are at school—in other words, a child's understanding that "My shoe box is there" constructs his or her feeling that "I was there," and clarifies his or her existence at school as a whole.

Of course, the stability of these environments does not mean they keep children exactly the same every day. They constantly exert influence on children to commence meaning construction in a variety of ways, because such environments always entail uncertainty and further possibility of meaning construction. For example, a shoebox in school that bears a child's name can facilitate a child's constructing of meaning from it quite different from the institutional one (e.g., "*I* like the girl whose shoe box was next to *mine*"). At first glance, mundane environments appear totally different from questions in interviews asking participants to reflect, or works of modern art that shake our understanding of the world and ourselves, but they still carry potential for meaning construction and clarification of ourselves reacting to them.

In these environments, naturally, an abrupt change of our relationship with our ordinary environment causes further meaning construction. In discussing sign-mediated processes of self-reflection, Gillespie (2007) listed four types of reason: "ruptures (problems with the subject-object relation), social feedback (where the other acts as a mirror), social conflict (in the struggle for recognition), and internal dialogues (through internalizing the perspective of the other on self)" (p. 689). Although Gillespie's discussion is aiming at deeper self-reflection, as illustrated by stories of English travelers to India, these dynamics also appear in our encounters with objects or others in daily settings. For example, a rupture presupposes a harmonious relationship with others or objects before it happens, and it occurs at some point of time when such a relationship changes. From this basic understanding, our loss of a favorite pencil or experiencing the sudden breakdown of a laptop full of precious data is a kind of rupture in our mundane environment, and can lead to our elaborated meaning construction concerning these events.

Reunions in Our Lives Show a Two-Sided Nature: An Inevitable Consequence of Modern Life and a Commodity to Be Consumed

In our daily lives, what exists at the base of the meaning construction described in the previous section are our repeated encounters, or *reunions,* with our objective and interpersonal environments, and what bring about equilibration and dis-equilibration are also often contained in these reunions. Such reunions are ubiquitous in our lives. Institutionalized settings such as school or workplace and intimate relationships in

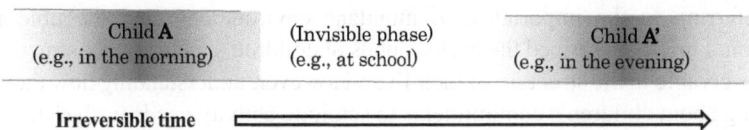

| Child **A** (e.g., in the morning) | (Invisible phase) (e.g., at school) | Child **A'** (e.g., in the evening) |

Irreversible time

Fig. 6.2 Model of a child's daily movement and his or her invisibility from a parent's perspective

our home show qualitative differences in what we expect will happen and what we are expected to do, and we transfer between these circumstances regularly. As discussed in Chap. 3, this boundary crossing experience in life makes the child's relational position unstable, and it brings about reunions as daily events.

If we look at this process focusing on the visibility of children, these movements produce a phase of their lives that is invisible to their parents, which constructs potential differences between who the child is in the morning before school and who he or she is after returning home (Fig. 6.2). Conversely, children's lives in their homes are invisible for teachers at school. In these transitions, meaning construction in conversation (Chap. 3) occurs upon the reunion of children with their mothers, and children's writings about their experiences (Chap. 5) can be considered as something *prepared* for children's reunions with their teachers or classmates.

Generally speaking, these reunions occur when we divide our lives (e.g., by going to school every day), as moments that characterize the structure of our lives. If we extend the length of separation and frequency of reunions, they can be seen to exist in various moments in life—e.g., family gatherings in holiday seasons, conference meetings, homecoming days—and most of them are closely related to the dissection of our lives in time and space. In addition to reunions after physical separation, we also experience *pseudo*-reunions across time using a variety of devices. For example, photographs or videos enable us to meet others in the past, even including ourselves in the past.

At the same time, this word "re-union" connotes that whoever (or whatever) meets there should return to a state of *unity*, and the concept of reunion here introduces the presupposition that opposes the division. In relation to this presupposition, affective value is attached to reunions, especially when unexpected or after very long separations. However, reunions are not necessarily the result of adverse separations. Considering the examples of a class reunion or parents eagerly taking photos of their children for their (pseudo-)reunion in the future, we actively arrange reunions that are not necessarily required for our lives.

Thus, reunion is not only the inevitable result of the division of our lives but also what we *consume* in society as a kind of commodity. This suggests that reunion exists in our lives with contrasting characteristics. In one aspect, it is an unavoidable by-product of the society we live in, wherein unity must be achieved *despite* divisions. On the other hand, it is what we expressly produce for our pleasure or affective experiences by *identifying* the divisions for which we do not care if there is no reunion.

Referring to the importance of mundane environments and the ubiquity of reunion, I briefly described the backgrounds of children's meaning construction that are observable in the structure of their lives. However, understanding how they work to bring about children's commitments to semiotic activity needs further discussion of its underlying dynamics.

The Foundation of Reunion: Two Dialectic Tensions

To understand the function of reunion in our lives, here I assume two types of dialectic tension— same <> non-same and visible <> invisible—that play an important role in this process. They are closely related to, or rather inseparable from, reunion and meaning construction. In the analyses of conversation and writings, I already discussed how the dialectic dynamics of our language lead to meaning construction (Chaps. 3 and 5). However, in contrast with the dialectic dynamics that are traceable in the progression of conversation or in writings, here I consider dialectics at a more abstract level not observable in the concrete traces of meaning construction.

Firstly, reunion involves the phases of *visible* and *invisible* as its foundation. In the flow of time, the reunion is the point at which invisible switches to visible, or at the boundary of two qualitatively different times, and this indicates reunion and (in) visibility are co-definitive. Valsiner (2007) discussed this type of triplet relationship using C. S. Peirce's discussion. As we see in Fig. 6.3, Peirce emphasized the unique character of the present that is very close to, or dependent on, both past and future but brought about in between them.

In his discussion concerning the triplet of past, present, and future, Valsiner described the function of signs in the present thus: "It is through the construction of signs—iconic, indexical, and symbolic—that the perceiving/acting organism faces the future. Cultural psychology assumes the act of *construction* of novelty by the organism, based on the resources of the given setting and the experiences of the past transported to the present (…)" (p. 130). This suggests the importance of the reunion as a unique point at which semiotic activities are promoted in relation to the invisible past and to cope with the future, from the perspective of parents. Mothers' eagerness to talk about their children's experiences may stem from this unique property of reunion.

Secondly, this tension concerning visibility brings about the dialectic tension of same <> non-same that also establishes the occurrence of reunion. Reunion is realized when we *create the illusion* of the sameness of whom or what we encounter, even if only a fragment of it. For example, it cannot be a reunion if I see someone on a bus whom I actually met 10 days ago but failed to recognize his or her sameness and thus the dialogue never occurs. However, a dramatic reunion can take place when we meet a classmate from elementary school after 40 years of no contact, though there remains only one aspect (e.g., his or her name) capable of proving the identity of this person who was just a child in the class. This easily causes a dialogical process to clarify who we were during the separation with the elaboration

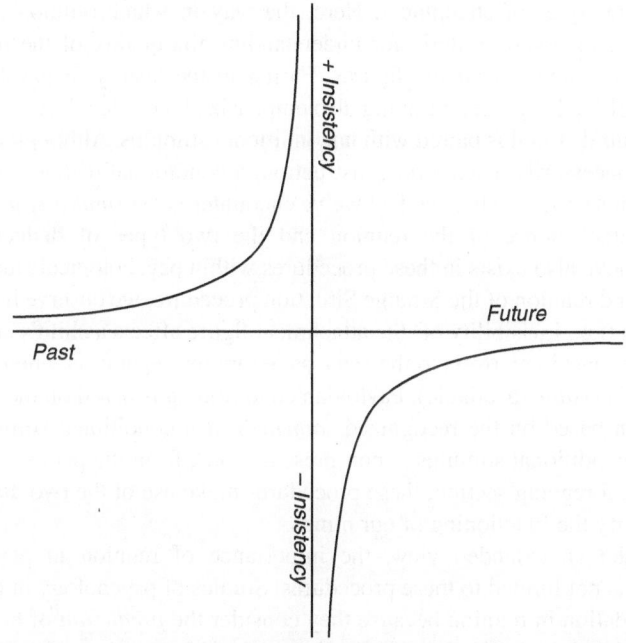

Fig. 6.3 Peirce's model of the relationship between the past, present, and future (Peirce 1892, p. 550)

or explication of the sameness and non-sameness of ourselves. In other words, the semiotic construction of sameness is not confirmation of the perfect identity, but rather the unification of the invisible past and the visible present.

Thus, reunion involves two types of dialectic tensions, and all of these things are co-definitive with each other. In the flow of time, they are always on the move and the exploration of sameness leads to further meaning construction. The affective value of reunion and our deliberate arrangement of it are also related to these two tensions. For example, in reunions after very long separation, the construction of a minor sameness out of similarity exists in stark contrast with extreme non-sameness (a strong tension of same <> non-same). This can make us experience strong affects as its derivatives, facilitating the construction of further sameness with each other amid the deluge of non-sameness.

Reunion, Prediction, and Psychology

Many theories of psychology also place the reunion and our reaction to it at the core of their theoretical frameworks. Looking at the theories concerning human development, the set of separation and reunion is at the core of the Strange Situation procedure (Ainsworth, Blehar, Waters, & Wall, 1978), which is widely used for clarifying the styles of attachment. Here, the way in which reunion is achieved serves as one of several criteria for understanding the quality of the relationship between infants and attachment figures. Earlier in the history of psychology, the framework of Pavlovian conditioning also emphasized the role of repeated encounters with neutral stimulus paired with unconditional stimulus. Although the reunion here is not necessarily a semiotic construction, a conditional response to a conditional stimulus appears when we feel we've encountered *the similar stimulus again.*

An interdependence of the reunion and the two types of dialectic tension discussed above also exists in these procedures within psychological studies. In the separation and reunion of the Strange Situation procedure, we observe how the separation from (i.e., invisibility of) the attachment figure affects a child's conduct and how the relationship recovers to the *same* as before the separation when the attachment figure is *visible* (available). Pavlovian conditioning is based on the production of a reaction based on the recognized *sameness* of a conditional stimulus, if the original, unconditional stimulus is non-present. Thus, from the perspective I introduced in the foregoing section, these procedures make use of the two dialectic tensions to clarify the functioning of our minds.

If we take an extended view, the importance of reunion in psychological discussions is not limited to these procedures. Studies of psychology in many areas have a foundation in reunion because they consider the *prediction* of behavior one of their crucial aims. Prediction of behavior works in our encounters with others or environments, and is closely related to the construction of sameness concerning self and others in our relationships. For this need, concepts of psychology (e.g., personality traits) bring us conceivable understanding of self and others (e.g., Today, he complained about his work *as always.*). Thus, many people feel a sense of relief when constructing the quasi-sameness of a person, including themselves, although in reality these psychological concepts have little ability to predict our behavior. Actually, using personality concepts for understanding is somewhat tautological: we "understand" the reason for a person's behavior that he or she has a tendency to behave in that way. However, this tautological understanding of one's personality constructs a plausible pair of expectation and realization, preparing the expectation to be realized, and we feel comfortable with that prediction ensuring the constructed sameness of self and others.

The Role of Dialogical Meaning Construction in Reunion

The discussion above shows that constructing the phantasmal sameness of self and others is inevitable in reunion, and as we saw in foregoing chapters, telling and writing personal stories are activities that work in the semiotic regulation of this same <> non-same tension. As is clear from the stories previously analyzed, this is not the construction of the precise sameness of others or ourselves, because one function of our personal stories is explaining what happened in the time that was invisible to our partner in the interaction. Stories clarify the non-sameness of us in the present and in the past. In other words, discovery of the sameness enables the reunion, but it always involves the non-sameness.

Although this may explain the role of our meaning construction in reunion, it still does not describe the *occasional* nature of the occurrence of such semiotic activities. If storytelling is a powerful way of regulating this same <> non-same tension of ours, why does it appear in non-regulated or non-predictable ways? In these complexities, we must understand that our actions do not follow a simple schema of causation and result, but are instead what occurs amid dialectic tensions that are always on the move, though this may sound like an abandonment of psychology's basic premise. Children's storytelling works within the tension of same <> non-same functions, in combination with other factors also related to this tension. In the next section, I attempt a somewhat bold leap to compare this framework—that is, our needs of regulating same <> non-same tension in reunions—with what we do when listening to music, in order to offer suggestions concerning the occurrence of meaning construction.

Reunion in Music: An Analogical Discussion on the Regulation of Reunion

Whether classical or pop, most musical compositions based on western music employ the variation of a "motif" or "theme" that appears repeatedly throughout the piece. Not only the tunes on the Billboard hit chart but also the masterpieces by J. S. Bach or L. van Beethoven rely on the reunion of the listeners and (variations of) a motif introduced in the beginning, or in the middle, of the flow of continuing movement of sounds. In other words, it is in our repeated encounters with this "almost the same but also non-same" melody that we experience our affective reaction to the entirety of a music piece—its meaning to us.

These reunions in the music we enjoy are commonly based on the order that dominates them. A theme in a musical piece also repeats in ways that fulfill our expectations, though many composers of music have challenged this order, as I discuss later. We are excited and satisfied when a favorite theme, whether romantic or brave, appears again at the climax, and we consider it strange if an intermezzo halts suddenly and the music switches to the climax directly. It is not only through such changes of mood but also in the proceeding of harmony and dynamics that we anticipate the arrival of a main theme. Although a piece may contain many transformations of tempo and tonality, what we listen to is basically dominated by organized tempo and standards dictating how one chord leads another, as textbooks of musical grammar tell us.

The system that dominates the reunion is also what makes us *understand* the reunion. In the history of music, especially in the nineteenth century, composers pursued novelty in their works by introducing harmonies that made novel impressions on listeners. Through these attempts, the format of music as dependent on major and minor keys was well elaborated—at the same time, the limitations of this system were already understood by composers (Griffiths, 2006). Despite this historical fact, most musical works circulating in contemporary societies rely heavily on this system with major or minor keys in their makeups. Even the latest hits, the music that people eagerly enjoy and feel is understandable, are just arrangements of the classical, standardized system that has been in use at least during the twentieth century.

The fact that many experimental music pieces are appreciated only by a few enthusiasts and that many people believe these pieces "very hard to understand" implies that the system described above is essential for many people in the repeated reunion with a melody. Historically, certain composers in the twentieth century—P. Hindemith and D. Shostakovich, for example—who experimented with new styles of music were oppressed by Hitler or Stalin (Griffiths, 2006). This illustrates how music in excess of expectations makes people confused and sometimes irritated. Thus, our meaning-making in music achieved through repeated encounters (reunions) with a short motif is comfortable when this is some arrangement of a ready-made, fundamental structure. This basic idea shows some affinity to the role of psychological concepts in our understanding of self and others in reunion as discussed in the previous sections, in that both of these serve to *fulfill our expectations*.

Suggestions from the Trials of Music History: A Focus on the *Openness* of Reality

Viewed from a commercial perspective, the order of music that controls the reunion and keeps it comfortable for us has demonstrated great success. However, from the beginning of the twentieth century, many composers aware of the limitations of the traditional system of music attempted to explore further possibilities. Atonality was an early example of this challenge, which rejected the order adopted for composing in the nineteenth century. John Cage (1912–1992), who once was a student of A. Schoenberg, was a composer who extended his attempts beyond the existing order of music, denying the authority of composers or players in varied ways. Extending from the discussion above, in which I sought to understand the psychological dynamics of everyday life as an analogue of music, here I inquire into a new possibility of psychological study referring to his method of composition.

Griffiths (1981) used the concepts of silence, contingency, and natural sounds to characterize Cage's explorations. First played in 1952, his well-known work <4'33">, in which a player or players play *tacet* (in silence) on stage, emphasizes not only the possibilities of silence as music but the existence of a variety of sounds in the environment or in our physical sensations (e.g., heartbeats) that still exist when there is no performance of traditional music (Griffiths, 1981). His eagerness to use many types of sound other than those of typical musical instruments is clear in his early compositions featuring a prepared piano that produced sounds from objects placed between the piano's strings. He also used atmospheric sounds, considered superfluous noise according to the accepted principles of music or concerts. His exploration to transcend the constraints of traditional music was not limited to the sounds he used, but extended to the way a composition is achieved by introducing coincidences in the composition process. Griffiths (1981) suggested that Cage's emphasis on coincidences and the unknown derived not from his personal preferences, but from his deep respect for our ordinary lives dominated by lack of control.

Cage's willingness to introduce contingency against the existing order that gives us the sense of predictability and the sense of sameness in reunion must be justified with our understanding of human action in transcending the restrictions of existing presuppositions. Here contingency can be understood as openness to what may happen in reunion. If I apply this idea to the mother-child conversation, reunion is open to a variety of possibilities concerning the sameness of the child. To illustrate this relationship, here I modify Fig. 6.2 as Fig. 6.4. In a reunion of a child with his or her family, there are demands for constructing the sameness of the child and family relationships as before: not only with family members but in the child himself or herself. This sameness exists in a dialectic tension with the non-sameness that becomes evident in the flow of time or through their experiences. This tension prevails in music also—that is, we anticipate the re-appearance of the same motif in an arrangement that leads to the finale of a piece. However, the tension of same <> non-same in real interaction is not controlled in this way but is instead open to a variety of possibilities, as Cage attempted to show us in his composition emphasizing the contingency and diversity of the sounds we hear in silence.

Here I consider the interaction and meaning construction in the mother-child conversation discussed in Chaps. 1 and 3 as one actual way to construct this sameness and non-sameness.

(From Excerpt 1.2)

1 Mo: What is Saito Taku [Mina's friend, boy] (yes) going to play in the theater performance? (1 s).
2 Mi: A bat. (2 s) And Mina [I play] a rabbit.

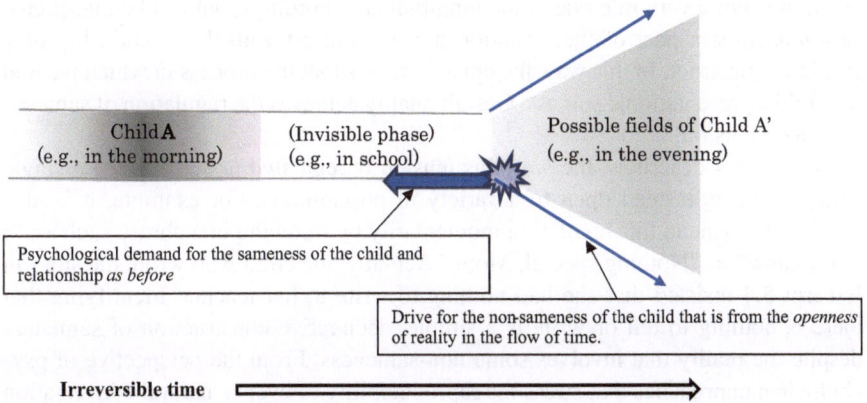

Fig. 6.4 Model of a child's daily movement and the tension of same <> non-same

3 Mo: In the dance by the rabbits? The bat? (1 s) [Does he appear in] Another dance?

4 Mi: After the bats, (uh hum) then maybe rabbits, (hmm) bunny rabbits.

5 Mo: Mimi, the bunny ... Oops [I guess I was] wrong, snow rabbits!

6 Mi: Mina, the snow rabbit xx [inaudible].

7 Mo: Mina is [You are] a moon rabbit, aren't you? (Oh, [you are] right) A yellow rabbit, aren't you?

8 Mi: [I'm] Not a snow rabbit. (1 s) xx [inaudible]?

9 Mo: A flower rabbit. (Wrong) Mina, the moon rabbit.

10 Mi: That's right. Sayuri [Mina's friend, girl] and Sada Miki [Mina's friend, girl] play flower rabbits, don't they? (yes) Iiyama Mina and Sanae [Mina's friend, girl] are, well, moon rabbits, two moon rabbits and (yes) the white rabbit is, well, Tano (1 s) Tanokura (yes) Tano ... Tanokura, yeah, Tanokura Nagisa [Mina's friend, girl].

11 Mo: Tanokura Nagisa.

12 Mi: And then, Matsuzaka Aika [Mina's friend, girl] (yes) Machida Mina, [Mina's friend, girl] (yes) [you] see?

13 Mo: Yes, [I] see.

14 Mi: Three girls do that together, right?

15 Mo: Yes, but Mina [you] play in two, don't you?

In this episode, the participants mentioned are the *same* members whom Mina meets every day in hoikuen. Referring to these regular members serves to construct the sameness of the child's experience, but their animal roles in their performance, which derive from the children's mundane environment, add to their non-sameness in comparison with the same children the previous day. In this fashion, they are regulating same <> non-same tension through this dialogical process. The relationship between the child and her mother is also implicated in this tension. In concrete terms, the child returns to her mother as one who needs her mother's help to show her the correct experiences; yet, in the latter half of the excerpt, she also attempts to assume a position to teach her mother experiences. This change of her position is not a very rale one in the longitudinal recordings, but can be interpreted as a *non-same* aspect of their relationship, in contrast with the relationship they regularly construct. In this way, the episode shows that the process in which we find the child's presentational self as a Gestalt quality achieves the regulation of same <> non-same tension.

As Fig. 6.4 describes, the way this tension is regulated is not fixed to a single solution, but is instead open to a variety of possibilities. For example, it is also possible to suspend this regulation momentarily by throwing in a phrase such as, "I don't know" or "Nothing special, Mom." Actually, the child who wrote the story in Excerpt 5.4 insisted that she had nothing to write to her teacher. Identifying that there is nothing to tell or write is a simple, declarative construction of sameness despite the reality that involves some non-sameness. From the perspective of psychological approaches that stress the reproducibility of events, natural conversation is thus unpredictable and does not fit within the framework, just as many experimental music pieces do not for us. However, our focus on the tensions at work in the reunion can explain the nature of such whimsical interactions and meaning construction.

Conclusion and Further Questions: Our Lives (and Our Research) Do Not Proceed like a Beautiful Music

Beginning from a question concerning the occasional emergence of the clearer presentational self in mother-child conversations and the fluctuations of children's writings, this chapter has focused on the concept of reunion and two types of dialectic tension closely related to it as what brings about and promotes the dialogical work of meaning construction. In children's environments that hold the potential for meaning construction, reunion exists both as a result of the unavoidable divisions of our lives and as a deliberate event to be consumed. As I have discussed, citing some theoretical frameworks, researchers of psychology have also discussed what occurs in reunion with someone or something to understand our minds.

These ubiquitous but crucial events in our lives have the potential to restructure our framework for understanding the process of meaning construction in conversation or writings. The function of our meaning construction in dialogical processes—i.e., the foundation of presentational self—is the regulation of the continuing tension of same <> non-same that derives from the tension of visible <> invisible. Although we are predisposed to expect smooth reunions, the kind we enjoy when we listen to music, our lives also involve a variety of coincidences and the tension of same <> non-same is resolved in various ways, as the attempts of Cage suggested to us. Researchers of psychology often suggest that our conduct stems from internal drives that make us move in a certain way. However, what we need to understand is the nature of tensions, same <> non-same and visible <> invisible, which are always in motion in the repeated reunion.

Dialogical meaning construction in storytelling works in these tensions and movements in combination with a variety of factors that appear coincidentally in our lives. For example, children's outward appearance provides a very strong foundation of their sameness in reunion, but it can also demonstrate their non-sameness (e.g., dirty shirts in the evening, different from cleanness in the morning). Children also retain their moods from the activities they experienced, which also work at the point that determines the talk <> not talk bifurcation, because it is a possible option to opt out temporarily from active meaning construction. It's significant that all these factors work toward the regulation of tensions and are not factors that disturb the *purposeful* activity of conversation or writing. With this understanding, it is difficult to predict exactly when and in what condition meaning construction occurs.

The history of music also tells us that, if we adopt a framework that considers meaning construction as what works on the basis of such tensions and coincidence, my exploration is accompanied by a problem concerning its understandability. In the world in which people, including researchers, are eager to understand self and others by uncovering their dispositions or simple rules that predict our acts, a discussion concerning the emergence of a clearer presentational self based on the accidental occurrence of meaning construction is hard to understand, or is even irritating. This is like when a piece of experimental music is considered too abstruse, or when a sudden expedient transformation of identity in a fairy tale is regarded as unreasonable. Thus, another question for us is how to correctly include the richness of a non-stable world—the kind we find in conversational interactions—into our theoretical thinking without this being rejected as a bizarre and meaningless discussion only enthusiasts could appreciate. In the following chapters, I will discuss this issue by elaborating two dialectic tensions introduced here, with a focus on their roles in the process of development across a variety of aspects.

Chapter 7
The Visibility of the Invisible: What *Propels* Meaning Construction in Our Lives

"But he hasn't got anything on," a little child said.

The Emperor's New Clothes
(H. C. Andersen, transl., Jean Hersholt)[1]

In Chap. 6, I suggested that at least two types of dialectic tension are present in the background of children's meaning constructions and the emergence of their presentational selves. The whimsical appearance of presentational selves can be attributed to the unpredictability generated by the tensions in our lives. Thus, elaborating the discussion concerning the selves emerging in meaning construction requires further understanding of how these tensions work.

This chapter focuses on one such tension: the tension of visible <> invisible, which is in close relationship with the reunion in children's lives. As I described, the (in)visibility of children often establishes the meaning construction that identifies or clarifies who they were while invisible to someone else (e.g., mothers, teachers). The influence and power of invisibility are not limited to such habitual activities, but are prevalent in our lives. For example, we have a presupposition that our future surely exists, though the future is invisible and open to various possibilities, including the possibility that we will not be in a position to experience it. Regardless, we still believe in our continuity and we use concepts such as responsibility for our actions, which is deeply related to our belief in our own continuity. This example illustrates how invisibility constitutes the semiotic construction of our lives, and suggests that invisibility exists in several aspects in our lives. In other words, the invisibility of a child for his or her parents during the daytime and the invisibility of our own selves 10 days in the future share the common quality that they do not exist here-and-now, immediately, but they differ in how they are invisible to us and what disrupts their visibility. To construct an integrative understanding concerning the dynamics of visible <> invisible tension, this chapter attempts a typological understanding of invisibility, drawing examples from psychological studies and our broader society.

---

[1] Retrieved from http://www.andersen.sdu.dk/vaerk/hersholt/TheEmperorsNewClothes_e.html

© The Author(s) 2019
K. Komatsu, *Meaning-Making for Living*, SpringerBriefs in Psychology,
https://doi.org/10.1007/978-3-030-19926-5_7

Invisibility by Substantial Obstacles: A Simple Pattern of Impediment

As mentioned in the previous chapter, psychological research exists in close relationship with reunion and the visible <> invisible tension, and many studies have discussed human development in relation to this. Among these, certain studies by J. Piaget focused on when and how children become able to understand the permanence of objects that are temporarily invisible to them. Infants' understanding of object concept (Piaget, 1955) was tested by covering an object with some obstacle (e.g., cloth). Piaget (1955) also showed the development of children's understanding from simple detection of a hidden object to their consideration of possible unseen movement of the object.

This well-known study suggests that one function of our mind lies in coping with the invisibility of objects from very early in our development, even before children start to use language well. Our actions in the world, both at the very local level and at the global level, depend on our understanding of a substantially hidden sphere. I *know* there is a kitchen next to the room where I work now, and I move there when I feel hungry. I also *understand* one of my colleague lives in a country in another hemisphere of the globe, and I send an email to him when I have something to tell him. Thus, in the foundation of our actions, there is often an understanding that there is something that we cannot find right now, due to physical obstacles or distances.

The word "visible" as I use it here refers to our visual perception in the first place. Yet the point is not to emphasize perceptual visibility but rather the physical distance and obstacles between the desired object and ourselves. In other words, invisibility here means the impossibility of finding something in our immediately perceptible environment. Although the technologies of communication now blur such obstacles and distances, our living in the physical world requires us to construct a worldview that includes physically hidden spheres.

The invisibility caused by physical distance and obstacles is related to time, as we learn in the first step of the calculation of speed. To confirm what is in the invisible side or space requires us to move there or make it move, and it takes time. Here the extension of our physical world involves time to transfer, and to find out everything in our surroundings simultaneously is impossible given the restrictions of time and space.

Invisibility Due to Physical Impediments and Meaning Construction

The concept of reunion discussed in the previous chapter mainly relies on this type of invisibility: i.e., the invisibility of children as viewed by others due to physical distance between them. In modern societies, institutions for children such as hoikuen or schools are usually clearly distinct from children's homes and there are substantial differences (distances) between them. Children's everyday movement between two places causes their re-appearance in the view of parents at home or teachers at school. However, this invisibility is also based on the social norms that require us to separate the private sphere from public institutions. If they have enough time, it is physically possible for parents to go and stay at the school to look at their children all the time. Although it may happen on some occasions, in most societies few parents will do this every day. Thus, the visible <> invisible tension concerning children is a result of both physical distance and socially shared rules. As I discussed in the foregoing chapter, the emergence of children's presentational selves in meaning construction awakens from this (in)visibility of children and it regulates another dialectic tension of the same <> non-same.

The meaning construction from invisibility also works on many occasions in our lives, and modern society controls what is visible and invisible to control our desire to know it. Accordingly, the secrecy adds value to the given content (Valsiner, 2007). For example, we do not wish to know what celebrities really do in their private lives; our not knowing the details of their private lives is essential for keeping them special and different from ourselves. The clearest example of this dynamic is in the religious discussions concerning the possibility of visualizing the ultimate other, as I discuss later. Thus, the visibility of others is related to the determination of who we are in relation to them.

From this perspective, constructing the physical invisibility of children by creating a childcare system or school system in society works to make it clear that each child has his or her own uniqueness that is distinct from family members. This was already suggested in the interview with mothers introduced in Chap. 4 (Excerpts 4.1 and 4.2), in which the mothers emphasized the independence of their children. In their discussion concerning young children's autonomy, Vuorisalo, Raittila, and Rutanen (2018) also reported parents' understanding that their children need a space outside the reach of parents. Thus, the invisibility of others is not simply the source of our curiosity or anxiety about what happened when we did not see them, but rather what brings about the otherness of children to parents or teachers. The mother-child conversation is thus established upon the generation of otherness of children for mothers (and vice versa) through invisibility. Conversely, children's writings in nikki journals are made when no one is visible for the children, yet it works for them to suppose the independence of themselves from others, and to create readers who are invisible for the moment.

Such meaning constructions also involve perspectives on the flow of time in relation to (in)visibility. When a mother and child talk about the child's experiences, they are visible to each other, but they must each consider the time when the child is invisible. The child who writes a story in nikki must *imagine* an invisible reader by presuming they will become visible in the future. Here the flow of time becomes an indispensable aspect of the dynamics. Children write personal stories at home, preparing for their meeting the following day: i.e., the moment the teacher becomes visible. In other words, the visible <> invisible tension that leads to the emergence of children's selves works through the flow of time, which also leads us to extend the concept of invisibility, as follows below.

Visibility by the Semiotic Extension of the World: An Extension from Physical Invisibility

When we expect an event to happen—i.e., to become visible—in the future, it is invisible for us at the time and will only be realized in the flow of time. Children *expect* to meet their teacher the next day, and it usually happens when they go to school. Given this realization of visibility in time, ways of achieving visibility are not limited to our physical movement in space. In school education, children's solving questions in mathematics exemplifies this process. When they are presented with a question, the answer is invisible to them and they are expected to solve it to achieve an answer that appears visibly on the paper.

The fundamental steps in these examples are similar: i.e., something becomes visible in the flow of time. Differences exist in how visibility is achieved. As Vygotsky (1986) emphasized in the mediating role of psychological tools, our language use is crucial to these processes to recognize objects otherwise invisible to us. Children's participation in educational practices involves such an orientation to make the invisible visible through their activities. Mastering calculations allows children to arrive at visible solutions, and children learn to read textbooks to say something hearable and understandable from otherwise meaningless sets of signs. In other words, school education is a systematic presentation of the invisible, from which children must construct something visible. In these activities, making the answer literally visible (e.g., writing into a notebook) is often recommended. Yet we also require children to have an *understanding* that enables visible answers. Thus, making something visible in such contexts means having a new understanding of it.

If I extend the tension of visible <> invisible in this way, visibility becomes more related to having an understanding of something latent. Returning to the examples of well-known tasks in developmental psychology, the discussion within research on "theory of mind" that is often represented by the false-belief task (e.g., Wimmer & Perner 1983) may exemplify this. In this procedure, children succeed in the task when they can reconstruct the false beliefs of another that are not apparent from (i.e., are invisible in) the episode presented to them.

Another Form of Invisibility for Promoting Children's Meaning Construction

Following the discussion in the former section, children describing their experiences in oral or written stories not only presents who they were, but also identifies what was formerly invisible. This orientation is clearer in children's writing of nikki as a task in elementary schools. Teachers who lead this activity are basically interested in children's experiences in their homes, and children's stories look like private products at first sight. However, as I discussed in Chap. 5, this activity was often intended to clarify the *meaning* of their experiences, or of their *lives*. In these contexts, educators placed emphasis on extending children's scope or visibility from the superficial viewing of what they saw to deeper meanings that they could possibly develop through their writings. For example, when a teacher recommends a child to write a story like Excerpt 5.5, in which the meaning of "milk jelly" extends into the past and the future, this represents the child uncovering a *meaning* of an object that does not necessarily appear just by looking at it.

This perspective on children clarifying invisible aspects of what they encounter was also emphasized in seikatsu-tsuzurikata education in the past, in which teachers often led children who lived in difficult circumstances. For example, they were expected to elaborate on their own or their family members' negative feelings in their lives, or to discover the meaning of work (Funabashi, 1996). In comparison with what is to be found in learning of arithmetic—i.e., one absolute correct answer—what becomes clear in writing personal experiences is basically dependent on the environment and characteristics of each individual child. However, when I consider the historical background, this activity shares the same orientation with what children perform in the classrooms: the clarification of what is invisible at first glance by their semiotic extension from the visible world.

The mother-child conversation about children's experiences involves a similar type of transition from invisible to visible. For example, a child and her mother collaboratively identify the reason why a bus is stopping on the street (Excerpt 1.1) and the name of a person whom they had met before (Excerpt 3.1). These examples are very simple but understandable as the clarification of what is invisible just by looking at the objects. It also suggests that at least a part of the meaning construction investigated through this monograph is, in a broader sense, semiotic extension for the clarification of the invisible that exists behind visible objects or events.

The Complex of Two Types of Invisibility and Meaning Construction

In our environment, the two types of visible <> invisible tension mentioned above coexist and interact to influence our conduct. On one hand, the switch of the visible to invisible, or the invisible to visible, that is generated by *physical* obstacles promotes our meaning construction concerning our environments and ourselves (e.g., children's going back and forth from school, the invisibility of celebrities' real lives). However, such meaning construction often focuses on the clarification of the invisible aspects that visible objects have, through semiotic extensions (e.g., discovering past and future interpersonal relationships in a milk jelly, or understanding why a bus stops in the neighborhood). Moreover, the result of this clarification is sometimes expressed in physically visible ways (e.g., writing an illustrated story in nikki).

These processes are essentially relational and relative. With physical invisibility, two people looking at one object from different perspectives will find different views depending on their positions, and the same applies to semiotic clarification. When children try to solve a calculation in mathematics, children do not see the correct answer at first but that answer is already visible for the teacher who asked the question. Even single individuals find a new perspective, different from the old one, when he or she finds a new meaning or aspect of an object viewed. Thus, the tension of visible <> invisible always exists with our position in relation to others or objects. It implies that the emergence of children's presentational self in meaning construction also means children clarifying the position from which they see something in their experience.

This relationship between visible <> invisible tension and the construction of our position, or our self, in relation to the object, is not limited to the area of child development or school education but is a very widespread phenomenon in our society. In these processes, the visible <> invisible tension often involves conflicts between the positions we take. To understand this process, history offers us a path to further inquiry, and the next section will make an explorative discussion on the role of invisibility in society by introducing examples in history.

The Visibility of the Invisible Other: Struggles in History

Our society has ample means for presenting the invisible other, which have been developed and maintained over generations. Visual symbols like icons or statues we see in museums are what people have long used to represent invisible others. Such symbolic images were not only for representing invisible and sacred referents, but also clarifying the worshippers' commitment to the community: that is, collective identity (Giesen, 2012).

As also discussed by Giesen (2012), such images are sometimes banned for their power to move people. Iconoclasms and the revival of depicted images for worship have recurred through history and are still observable even now. These things that sought to present the invisible objectively worked powerfully on our mind and our conduct, and our orientation concerning how to present them has long been the cause of conflict. The history of Christianity is filled with attempts to find a way of visually depicting Christ, and many figures were based on a variety of associations and allegories (Okada, 2009). Although the objects we find in museums or churches still display enormous variety in their styles, they are the results of convergence constructed through history.

In these trials concerning religious themes, some motives are depicted with values shared in society and desired by many people. For example, at least from my perspective, the Virgin Mary we find in churches or museums is often described as the embodiment of beauty and nobility. However, people's experiments always involve opposing orientations. Discussions concerning medieval history describe artists as sometimes depicting the invisible other as unusually ugly, absurd monsters potentially capable of evoking strong emotional reactions and desire to flee from them, as well as curiosity about them. In his inquiry into depictions of monsters in the Middle Ages, Williams (1996) interpreted the appearance and development of monsters as follows:

> In the Middle Ages and other periods and cultures in which the monster flourished, the existence of a transcendent, ineffable reality superior to and paradigmatic of mundane reality was undoubted. The representation of this essentially unrepresentable reality was the goal of both philosophy and art. The limitations of discursive language seem to have been recognized almost from the beginning of philosophical thought, and the general nature of those limitations identified as language's need for a sign to represent a truth, which sign, by its nature, remains different and distinct from what it signifies. (p. 85).

This understanding suggests that the depictions of invisible objects were people's attempts to extend their visibility of the world. However, because of the indefinite nature of the object in these explorations, these attempts are never-ending, and people always wished for the renewal of these presentations in history. In addition, as the iconoclasms of history show, these explorations are not constrained to one linear direction from invisible to visible.

Regulation of Visibility for Construction of the Self

Attempts to depict the invisible, ultimate other in figures or pictures have been often in conflict with dogma that argues such depictions are impossible. This conflict was sometimes followed by the destruction of figures, yet backlash was also experienced from the strong desire to have concrete images. Major swings between these two poles are evident: for example, in the eighth to ninth century of Byzantine history, which shows repeated iconoclasms and revival of icons. If we consider visibility in a purely pictorial sense, these events can be understood as very large-scale, long-term adjustments of visible <> invisible tension. However, from the current discussion that includes both substantial and semiotic clarification of the invisible, they constitute disputes not about the possibility of visibility, but about the form of visibility.

Under complicated conditions, the control of invisibility becomes more complex. For example, Jonckheere (2012) discusses the characteristics of a painting by the Flemish painter Adriaen Thomasz Key (1554–1599) that was completed in 1575. It depicts the Mary Magdalene, and in a sense, this is a visualization of the saint. However, the painting is without iconographic symbols and contains many characteristics that precisely follow the description of Mary Magdalene by one of the leading Calvinists of the age. Thus, the painting clearly reflects the sway between Catholicism and the Protestant iconoclastic fury (the *Beeldenstorm* in 1566) and demonstrates very fine control of visibility, capable of coping with the kind of visibility that society demanded.

The worship of the crypto-Christians in Japan during the period when Christianity was prohibited in Japan (1614–1873) is another example. After accepting the

Catholic mission in 1549, many people in Japan, including some lords, converted to Catholicism. Although the propagation of and worship in the Catholic faith was later prohibited, some people on the western end of the Japanese archipelago maintained their Christian faith in secrecy for some 260 years, publicly behaving as non-Christian.[2] Under suppression, they kept various pictures and figures for their worship (e.g., crosses, statues of the Virgin Mary), but these were strictly hidden or blended with figures of Buddhism.[3] In this way, they owned *visible* objects that worked in special ways to limit the people capable of understanding their meaning. These examples show that control of visible <> invisible tension lies not only in the possibility of describing, but also in the possibility of accessing the visible objects.

This construction of a variety of visibilities of the indefinite other is also seen in the positioning of the self in relation to the other. Okada (2009) introduced the idea that Christ was a *mirror*, referring to the belief in early Christianity that the figure of Christ emerges in different ways depending on the knowledge and the virtue of the viewer. In some sense, it is similar to Hans Christian Andersen's story "The Emperor's New Clothes" in which everyone except for one child does not wish to be seen as stupid and thus *sees* the new clothes. This fundamental relationship between the invisibility of the indefinite other and ourselves is even applicable to the meaning construction discussed in this monograph. In concrete terms, the way that others (e.g., friends at hoikuen, family members) become visible serves as a *mirror* that reflects the self of the child who engages in meaning construction.

Conclusion: Ambivalence of Visibility

In this chapter, I discussed the tension of visible <> invisible in relation to the processes of meaning construction investigated in the former chapters. On the border of visibility and invisibility, the process that leads the emergence of presentational self occurs. Considering what brings about (in)visibility, this tension is discussed from two perspectives. One is the visibility controlled by some substantial impediment. Although obstacles that prevent our viewing may be physical, this also involves social customs and is inseparable from the flow of time. It suggests another type of tension that is accomplished by semiotic processes. I considered the writing of nikki stories one such attempt in school education. In our lives, these two types of invisibility are related to each other; rather, they act as a composite to promote our meaning construction.

I also extended the relationship between (in)visibility and meaning construction and suggested that the types of visibility concerning objects stipulate who we are in our relationships with them. This process is fundamental to religious attempts to

---

[2] The forms of worship practiced among them differed, depending on the areas in which they lived. There is also a discussion concerning the understanding of their worship in relation to orthodox Catholicism. See Komatsu (2017) for further discussion.

[3] For pictures of concrete examples, see Komatsu (2017, p. 24, Figure 1)

depict the objects of our worship, and a very brief look at the history provides us various ways to construct visibility and our positions. Their orientation toward visibility positions worshippers in relationship with the ultimate other. Although the goal differs between religious practices and our everyday conduct, how we look at others serves to construct our observing selves in relationships, and the discussion here converges with the discussion of the presentational self that emerges in multiple relationships with others.

We are highly ambivalent in our relationship with visible <> invisible tension. Some well-known tasks in developmental psychology cited here emphasized the importance of understanding hidden and invisible objects, which can serve as an index of development. Further, in our everyday lives we naturally wish to extend what we can see, both physically and semiotically. However, these desires for visibility are gratified or approved because there always exist new invisibilities. For example, our society routinely needs surveillance cameras for visibility of events, but we also demand our privacy. In these ways, we constantly need and construct invisibility that competes with visibility. In other words, meaning construction begins with supposing something is invisible: for example, "My child is invisible to me now" or "The meaning of their experiences is invisible to the pupils." This again suggests that the development must be understood in relation to dialectic dynamics, and I investigate these dynamics from a different perspective in the following chapter.

Chapter 8
The Dialectic Dynamics of Same <> Non-Same and Human Development

In addition to the role of visible <> invisible tension, the discussion in "Reunion with Others: Foundations of the Presentational Self in Daily Lives" also suggested that the meaning construction discussed in this monograph is essentially a regulation of same <> non-same tension concerning children. Previously, we observed young children telling detailed stories of their experiences to their mothers, and elementary school children writing the details of their interactions in nikki journals addressed to their teachers. Now I will consider these children's works in the construction of their sameness and non-sameness, both for others and themselves.

This tension is ubiquitous in children's lives. In the flow of irreversible time, children are considered basically the *same* person by the adults around them. However, their meaning construction sometimes constructs a detailed presentation that elaborates the non-sameness that they achieve in their lives, in contrast with the illusion of sameness that others have of them. This understanding shows that development is never a phenomenon presented via the change of several indices, but rather what occurs in the fluctuation based on the preservation of sameness and the emergence of non-sameness. In this fluctuation, constructing a model to predict the occurrence of a certain meaning construction is difficult; what I was able to do was discover several characteristic episodes within a large volume of qualitative data to illustrate what *possibly* happens. Moreover, these meaning constructions are achieved at the microgenetic level, and may have no direct effect on development at the ontogenetic level.

This difficulty of prediction concerning meaning construction also indicates the need to understand the same <> non-same tension that is at the foundation of our development. Although many of us very naturally believe that our material or social environments are stable, we constantly inhabit the non-sameness of them. In this process, non-sameness is not only the result of development, but also a ground that leads to further development. Thus, to elaborate the nature of development I have pursued through this monograph a little further, here I will add a very short discussion concerning the dynamics of same <> non-same tension, which has already been pointed out by the founders of developmental psychology.

© The Author(s) 2019
K. Komatsu, *Meaning-Making for Living*, SpringerBriefs in Psychology,
https://doi.org/10.1007/978-3-030-19926-5_8

The Dialectic Tension Concerning Sameness as Ubiquitous Dynamics

In our daily lives, we presuppose the sameness of our environment and of ourselves as the foundation of our conduct. We ordinarily understand that we live in the same house as yesterday, sleep in the same bed, and meet with the same family members. On this understanding, we also assume the stability of our selves, which plays an important role in our lives. In this way, our construction of the sameness of ourselves and our environment works with our belief in the existence of the invisible future (Chap. 7) to validate our roles in society.

Conversely, when we focus on the microgenetic aspects of our conduct, both ourselves and our environments are not exactly the same as they were even 1 second ago. For example, when we spend time in our house, we are often moving inside the house and physically not in the same position. Even when we watch TV on the couch, our eyes move to follow the movements onscreen. This can be generalized as "in the movement between *being in* the current setting and *striving out* of that very same setting" (Valsiner, 2007, p. 127). The setting itself is also constantly on the move. For example, the house we live in seems to look the same at all times, but sunlight from the windows is always moving, gradually changing the view inside the room. Thus, we construct a stable world and stable selves despite the fact that almost everything is constantly changing. In other words, our environments have *similarity*, not the exact sameness.

This presupposition of the sameness of people and environments also applies to studies of developmental psychology. Although many describe the changes in our actions (i.e., performance in a given task) along the flow of time, this does not assume that the person became a totally different person. These studies also rely on the sameness of the tasks or questions used in the data collection. The developmental or inter-individual differences among reactions are discussed in relation to tasks understood as remaining the same during multiple uses of them by the researchers, and the sameness of the people who gave these performances. In this way, change is often understood only in relation to sameness.

Considering these dynamics, the processes of meaning construction analyzed in the former chapters are the microgenesis that competes with the construction of the sameness. As I discussed in Chap. 6, these processes are closely related to participants' recognition of the sameness of themselves in reunion. However, this recognition exists in relation to non-sameness: that is, the conversation or writings concerning children's experiences describe what makes them different from before. Thus, the presentational self is what appears in the area of *similarity* constructed by children and their relationships with their environments.

Focus on the Repetition and Its Amplitude

Though it is difficult to predict precisely what will happen in these dynamics (Chap. 6), the concept of similarity gives us access to the nature of development at the microgenetic level. In discussing pragmatics, Sovran (1992) focused on the relationship between similarity and sameness, suggesting that many subtypes of similarity, denoted by the various ways of description (e.g., imitation, repetition) "display a certain tension between '*oneness*' and '*separate individuation*'" (p. 335). He also discussed the critical role of similarities in our recognition as "they help us to leave the safe ground of known, labeled, categorized terms, and *to expand our knowledge and language to newly discovered areas*" (p. 342, italics added). Thus, similarity is what works in the middle of the same <> non-same tension we undergo every day, and Sovran's discussion again suggests that the development is what happens as our non-sameness also brings about our similarity in time.

Looking at the emergence of the presentational self in conversation and writings considering the dynamics above, part of the background that constitutes this phenomenon is the repetition of similar activities in similar environments. In concrete terms, repeated reunions offer similar settings for children (e.g., talks during car rides, writing stories in a notebook). These similar settings include a variety of minor non-sameness (e.g., what they see from the car window, what the child ate before writing a story) and they give the meaning construction *fluctuation* in repetition, as I discussed using the metaphor of waves on the beach, in which a very high wave is occasionally seen (Chap. 3) (Fig. 8.1).

This is typically observable in the nikki of third- and fourth-grade children (Chap. 5). They often repeatedly write the same type of story describing what happened in a time sequence. In this repetition of writing in *similar* settings, they construct the meaning of their experiences in *similar* ways. However, within the amplitude of similarity, there sometimes appears an extension of meaning construction that marks a peak in the fluctuation. Although the mother-child conversation is more complex in its repetition because there are two participants engaging in mean-

Development of meaning (e.g., complexity) -> Achieved **non-sameness** of the children

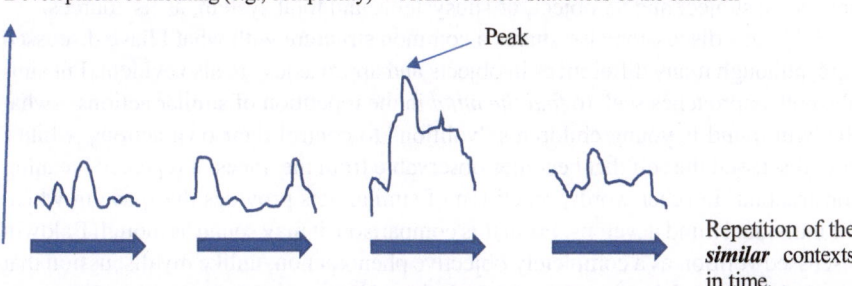

Peak

Repetition of the *similar* contexts in time.

Fig. 8.1 Development of meaning in repetition

ing construction with their own experiences, a similar foundation for meaning construction exists in its repetition.

This suggests two types of similarity, or same <> non-same tension, at work in the activities I have analyzed: one in the similarity of contexts and another in the similarity of children achieved in meaning construction. The episodes I picked up from massive amounts of data were typical ones at the extreme ends of fluctuation in everyday dialogue. This also shows the possibility of understanding development by looking at the repetition, fluctuation, and peaks that appear in them, and not relying on quantitative indices that often overlook such small changes by calculating average values.

Our *mind* Emerges and Develops in the Similarity of Behaviors

The perspective of seeking development within the tension of same <> non-same appeared very early in the history of modern psychology. Baldwin (1892) discussed the emergence of volition in young children, focusing on the role of persistent imitation that appears when infants repeatedly try to grasp something, for example. In his framework, persistent imitation differs from simple imitation in two aspects: "a comparison of the first result produced by the child (movement, sound) with the suggesting image of 'copy' imitate, i.e., deliberation" and "the outburst of this complex motor condition in a new reaction, accompanied in consciousness by the attainment of a monoideistic state (end) and the feeling of effort" (p. 286). This suggests that Baldwin believed the foundation of the emergence of our mental functioning lies in the repetition and the comparison of *similar* actions.

In the construction of developmental psychology in history, theoretical thinking after Baldwin often considered the opposition of same <> non-same, which leads to the repetitive occurrence of similarity or difference, to be the foundation of development. This dialectic idea played an important role in Vygotsky's development of the concept of the zone of proximal development (Valsiner & van der Veer, 2014). The concept of equilibration by Piaget (1985) also considered negation in the interaction between a subject and an object, or subsystems and total system, as its sources.

Baldwin's discussion also shares a common structure with what I have discussed here, although many differences in objects and approaches are also evident. Put simply, both approaches seek to *find the mind* in the repetition of similar actions—what Baldwin found is young children's "volition" to control their own actions, while I have discussed the self that becomes observable from the traces of repeated meaning construction. In other words, repetition of similar acts provides the space in which the individual mind develops. From this comparison, it may sound as though Baldwin discussed volition as a completely objective phenomenon, unlike my discussion that stressed the role of the observer who finds the self in meaning construction. However, here I point out the existence of Baldwin's own perspective, which attempted to find the function of mind in children's repeated movements and their reactions to them. In this aspect, Baldwin was also an observer who interpreted children's acts.

The level of non-sameness that triggers a new starting
point of fluctuation

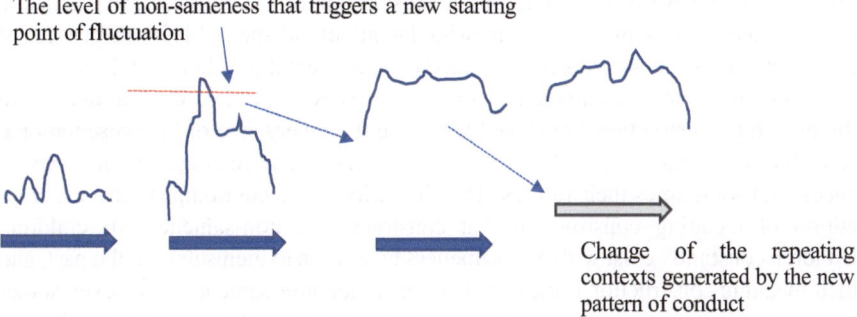

Change of the repeating
contexts generated by the new
pattern of conduct

Fig. 8.2 Construction of new types of fluctuation

This focus on similarity in repetition as a source of development of mind suggests the need to include how we behave over and over again in our daily lives. Although not clearly described in my inquiries, the discussions by Baldwin or Piaget suggest changes in such repetition can generate further, clearer changes in our own acts, as hypothetically depicted in Fig. 8.2. In this process, the peak in fluctuation works to set a new starting point that leads to another fluctuation, and this change also gradually creates the alteration of repeating contexts that enables another fluctuation.[1] The repetition in our daily lives looks like reiterations of mundane, conventional conduct, but it has the potential to serve as the starting point for qualitatively different action. In other words, movements of data that are often considered errors, and either controlled or canceled in the accumulation of mass data, are actually what leads the development.

However, not only quantitative approaches to development but also many qualitative inquiries fail to pay attention to the repetition of everyday activities or the fluctuation of what is narrated in interviews, except for a few studies (e.g., Potter and Wetherell 1987) focusing on the instability of attitudes observable in interviews. This tendency shows psychology's basic orientation toward presupposing the stability of ourselves and trying to reveal development using one-time questions, including interviews for qualitative analysis. These studies miss an important presupposition of development.

Conclusion: Spring Up in Repetition, Happen to Be Self

The discussion in this short chapter added some elaboration of the same <> non-same tension that is involved in the foundational structure that promotes the meaning construction (Chap. 6). In clear contrast with another opposition, the visible <>

---

[1] This discussion is based on the discussion by Ujiie (1996) that inquired into the nature of development citing a variety of theories, including chaos theory with non-linearity, and many records of observation and interviews.

invisible, which we often intentionally seek to control or construct, the dialectic tension concerning sameness is somewhat latent but indispensable in the process of development, as the theories that founded developmental psychology tell us.

This dialectic that actually appears as similarity works in two ways in relation to the meaning construction I analyzed to enable the emergence of the presentational self. One is the similarity of the contexts in which children re-construct their experiences, and sometimes their futures. The similarity of the environment provides repetition of meaning construction that constructs the non-sameness of children. Children constantly exist with non-sameness in relation to themselves in the past, and their meaning construction is the clarification of their non-sameness. However, somewhat contradictory, this is achieved within the range of similarity they maintain.

Under this half-restricted condition, meaning construction *springs up* again and again in the dialogical dynamics with others in different modalities: sometimes in reality (i.e., conversation) and sometimes presumed by children (i.e., nikki writing). In these activities, our orientation toward sameness can avoid the construction of non-sameness by saying or writing "Nothing new" or "Good as always," but there sometimes appears an upsurge that shows a clearer presentational self. In other words, some moves within the repetition of similar meaning constructions *happen to be found* as children's selves with uniqueness.

This perspective may befit the approach of a therapist more than a researcher. For example, Utsumi's (2013) inquiry as a clinical psychologist caring for children in homes for abused children describes several very brief but impressive moments in which children reveal contemplative comments about themselves despite broad-ranging aggression and emotional confusion. These are not necessarily related to the drastic changes in their conduct, but can be understood as events that constitute the therapist's understanding of the child as a whole. Such moments surely happen and can be important in therapeutic relationships, but these are not clarified by ordinary psychological methods.

The discussion here still does not predict when meaning construction will develop, but instead describes the very fundamental dynamics in which it occurs. Considering the process here including the dialectics of visible <> invisible, both meaning construction and human development are better understood when we describe these together with their instability, from a subjective perspective that focuses on specific moments.

Chapter 9
The Presentational Self and Meaning Construction *in Our Lives*

In this concluding chapter, I make a conceptual summary of the presentational self in meaning construction as discussed throughout my exploration, and I attempt to briefly point out its newness for our understanding the self in our lives. Although I constructed my discussion with a focus on the interactions in which children partici-pate, this review takes a wider view to understand the functioning of *our* minds in general.

Since its beginning, psychology has kept asking study participants, including children, *who they are,* in various ways. Some asked them about it directly, while others inquired into our thinking with a variety of tasks and inventions. In doing so, we psychologists have been constructing a static understanding of the mind, including our self-representations or self-understanding. We also invoke high scientific purpose as the reason why we *must* ask these questions. Some of us claim to do that for basic understanding of human nature, while others stress the practical need to save children from undesirable results of development. Psychology always needs rationales for our questioning and understanding of the mind, and we are used to such pairings of reason and result (or understanding). Yet understanding of this kind is a static representation of the self, assumed to exist in individuals as an internal entity, or of personality features with mystical causal properties (e.g., I am shy because of my introversion).

Of course, questions are being asked all the time. Our daily lives are sites where other people ask us many questions, and we also ask questions of others. However, these questions do not necessarily accompany clear intentions; sometimes they stem from serious interest in another's experiences, but some are just killing time before dinner, although this may also function perfectly well in our relationships. Here the absence of any reason paradoxically implies the legitimacy of questioning in our lives. We are asked questions because our lives are the places in which we are permitted to be asked, even though we do not necessarily have to answer. Our lives are the site of dialogical interaction and negotiation that has been constructed throughout history, and we understand each other through these interactions.

© The Author(s) 2019
K. Komatsu, *Meaning-Making for Living*, SpringerBriefs in Psychology,
https://doi.org/10.1007/978-3-030-19926-5_9

The inquiries in this monograph are the extension of these understandings in daily dialogues made without academic reason. For this reason, the discussion here is not directly related to practical advice that one might use. However, the data shown here exemplify the process by which meaning construction is made and "who children are" becomes clearer in their lives. Although these analyses lack some objectivity in their procedure and do not guarantee reproducibility, they construct a new framework to grasp *development,* microgenetically and ontogenetically, in relation to the dynamics that require and establish meaning construction.

A Relational View on the Self in Meaning Construction

To discuss the self and meaning construction in children's lives, I first proposed three fundamental orientations for my inquiries, considering the characteristics of our daily interactions (Chap. 1). These are the focus on continuous dynamics of meaning construction; consideration of the observer who understands what is achieved in the interaction; and the avoidance of over-reliance on reproducibility as an assurance of the findings. None of these fit with the presuppositions of contemporary psychology, but they help figure out the nature of daily lives.

This approach to children's selves resonates with explorations by researchers who were active over 70 years ago. In the development of psychology, there surely was a tradition that tried to understand the emergence of meaning as a *presentation in our mind* that was constructed from a variety of objects working as a whole (Chap. 2). To understand this process in children's meaning construction, I took the basic framework of the semiotic approach of cultural psychology (Valsiner, 2007, 2017) that attempts to understand the emergence of psychological data as the result of movement of the agencies of meaning construction (i.e., study participants, researchers). The analysis of mother-child conversations in this framework clarified how young children and their mothers elaborate their shared field of meaning relying on the potential of the concepts or proper nouns they introduced into the field, which I described using the dialectic dynamics denoted as **A <> non-A** (Chap. 3). It is in this process that the presentational selves of children emerge in *our* understanding, looking at the interaction.

This approach to the self is different from recent psychological research into the self, which often uses fixed questions to identify self-representation or self-understanding presupposed as an internal entity. However, the model of the presentational self insists that the pairs of questions and answers that constitute such pseudo-scientific reports are one subtype of the dialogues that enable the emergence of the presentational self, although awkwardly perverted and restricted (Chap. 4). In other words, the self is somehow appearing in *every* dialogue we participate in, even when we say nothing about our experiences.

My approach has focused on how the "I" of the children emerges in interaction, in clear contrast with empirical research in the past that attempted to draw out the

"I" as something demanded in response to questions posed by researchers. Although a somewhat hackneyed phrase, this suggests the self emerges, totally dependent on the other(ness) that constructs the dialogical relationship. In concrete interactions for meaning construction, there is no *generalized* other.

Dialogical Process in Meaning Construction and the Emergence of the Self

The analysis of children's writings as an application of the presentational self concept clarified the role of others in meaning construction in detail through their non-attendance in meaning construction (Chap. 5). Because of the absence of concrete others who collaboratively extend the shared field of meaning *on site*, children in the third and fourth grades often used stereotyped ways of meaning construction to enumerate events or objects they encountered. However, children also extended these by introducing a variety of dialogues into the process.

These examples also showed how the self becomes clearer for a person who describes his or her experiences. This involves multiple types of dialogical relationships with others, which differ depending on how conversation is achieved. In these dynamics, the child who writes his or her personal stories is also able to find the self in the result of meaning construction, presumably clearer than in conversation, which is not accompanied by visible traces.

The others appearing in meaning construction have distinctive roles. The importance of self–other comparison or interpersonal relationships in the construction of the self has already been pointed out in existing research. In addition to these discussions, current analyses have showed that others work powerfully as promoters of meaning construction that potentially drive a variety of extensions of meaning (e.g., Excerpt 3.2), or to trigger the child's strong reactions and give him or her clearer focus on details (e.g., Excerpt 5.6). Thus, the emergence of the presentational self always accompanies dialogue with others, and this process has its foundation in the structure of our lives.

Dynamics of Daily Lives that Enable Meaning Construction

Once we understand these dialogical processes, the question that remains is how these processes occur, proceed, and re-occur in our lives. This question was not asked in existing psychological studies, because these basically involve researchers posing questions to participants, or otherwise asking participants to talk about something that fits the purpose of the research.

My inquiry into children's selves first discussed the relationship between reunions in children's lives and their meaning construction. The phenomenon of reunion is ubiquitous in our lives, and it is not just an occasion for casual conversation. As is observable in many well-known procedures in psychology, reunion is deeply related to the functioning of our minds and depends on two types of dialectic tension in our lives: visible <> invisible and same <> non-same. It is difficult for us to control or predict how reunion is achieved, but these dialectic tensions are the keys to further understanding the process (Chap. 6).

The dialectic tension concerning visibility is related to both the physical and social construction of the world we live in. Basically, we have a tendency to identify the hidden both by our movements in the physical world and by semiotic extensions, yet we are somehow ambivalent in our relationship with invisibility. As is clear from history, we *need* invisibility because we need to construct ourselves by making something else visible to us (Chap. 7). On the other hand, the tension of same <> non-same is a latent dynamic that enables development in the area of *similarity* (Chap. 8). Although this study focused on the microgenesis of meaning, this perspective suggests inquiries into a wide range of developments occurring in the fluctuations of our actions.

The Indivisibility of Relationship, Meaning Construction, and the Self

Ever since the definition of the self by James (1890), inquiries of psychology have presupposed the self to be what exists inside *independent* persons. Although the theorists of symbolic interactionism considered the roles of others in the emergence of the self (e.g., Mead, 1934), they still described processes attributable to individuals. Harter (1999)'s discussion below suggests the powerful effect of James's perspective on psychology over a century ago, even 20 years after this discussion was made. In other words, most psychological studies of the self can be included in the framework explained here.

> In James, therefore, we find many themes that anticipate contemporary issues about the self. First and foremost is the distinction between "I" and "Me" selves, which has become of paramount importance to developmental psychologists. James' multidimensional, hierarchical view of the Me-self has been modernized in recent treatments of the self-structure, where investigators have sought to examine the particular relationships among global and domain-specific self-evaluations. Moreover, the potential conflict between different Me-selves that James observed has served as a springboard to contemporary interest in the construction of multiple selves. (pp. 16–17)

The discussion in this monograph emphasizes the self in the *indivisible* complex of relationships, meaning construction and the self, not in *individuals*. Although existing studies always emphasize the importance of interpersonal relationships that have huge effects on the self, it might even sound contradictory that we find the self *not* in the individual but in relationships. To exemplify this basic conclusion, once more I will introduce the cast of a story written by a great Danish author.

> So off went the Emperor in procession under his splendid canopy. Everyone in the streets and the windows said, "Oh, how fine are the Emperor's new clothes! Don't they fit him to perfection? And see his long train!" Nobody would confess that he couldn't see anything, for that would prove him either unfit for his position, or a fool. No costume the Emperor had worn before was ever such a complete success.
>
> "But he hasn't got anything on," a little child said.
>
> "Did you ever hear such innocent prattle?" said its father. And one person whispered to another what the child had said, "He hasn't anything on. A child says he hasn't anything on."
>
> "But he hasn't got anything on!" the whole town cried out at last.
>
> The Emperor shivered, for he suspected they were right. But he thought, "This procession has got to go on." So he walked more proudly than ever, as his noblemen held high the train that wasn't there at all.
>
> (transl. Jean Hersholt)[1]

The context is filled with the tension of visibility and invisibility. As I discussed in Chap. 7, almost everyone attempts to *see* the new clothes to befit his or her position (i.e., the construction of their selves). They are constructing relationships with the object and the Emperor and thus becoming obedient servants or good, clever citizens. In this way, their role or who they are in society is closely related to the meaning construction. However, the child who reveals the deception best exemplifies my discussion. Perhaps in a dialogue with his or her father, the child constructs a new meaning in relation to what was observed. Though the father tries to exercise his power by framing this as "innocent prattle," thus attempting to *position* his child as one who knows nothing, the meaning construction clarifies the child's *uniqueness* both in relation to others (i.e., the adults around the child) and what is observed.

The self here appears in the meaning construction and in the relationships, and *we* find it. If we could interview the child about what he or she thinks about his or her self, it is quite plausible that the child would not mention innocence or honesty, at least prior to the event. If the child was to make the same comments while watching the broadcast of the procession on television, assuming such a thing existed, the ultimate end would be different, because the meaning construction would be made and would function in an environment distant from the site. Accordingly, the child's presentational self is not what the child describes about the self, nor something that constantly and stably exists inside the child, but rather what we find in the meaning construction in context and in the configuration of persons and objects as a result of the meaning construction.

---

[1] Retrieved from http://www.andersen.sdu.dk/vaerk/hersholt/TheEmperorsNewClothes_e.html

The story also describes the same <> non-same tension and development. From an objective viewpoint, the procession is almost the same until the end of the story. The Emperor also keeps his self-understanding as an emperor. However, the child's meaning construction has changed what the procession may lead to: from the rise of the Emperor's authority to the undermining of it. In a world that seeks to maintain its sameness, *some* meaning construction clarifies the self in relationships and can also trigger huge developments.

As the final point, this monograph itself is an act of presentational self, in which *you* find *my* self. In my efforts to find out how to give new meaning to the concept of the self, I went through a wide range of conversations with theories and empirical evidence. Yet I surely know that the Emperor's procession keeps going on. Or maybe not?

Commentary 1
An Original Contribution With Great Potential

Mogens Jensen

I am happy to write a comment on Komatsu's text which I find very interesting and where I see many potentials to develop in the future. In the following, I will start by characterising my way of understanding the theory and then elaborate on some of the aspects. I will continue by pointing to some topics within applied psychology where I see this contribution as very productive and finally point so some aspects that in my view would be interesting to investigate in a future development of the theory.

Presentational Self and Cultural Psychology

In cultural psychology as this is characterised in the Yokohama manifest (Valsiner et al. 2016) the starting point and foundational axiom is to see humans as meaning making and embedded in a culture. I understand meaning making as processes where experiences with the environment are analysed and elaborated with the aim of creating an understanding by which the world and life becomes orderly and predictable at least to some degree. It suffices with local and delimited understandings for a certain environment and/or situations and they do not necessarily have to be consistent with each other as long as they help us handle the situations we experience. These understandings are necessary in order to feel (relatively) safe and to enable intentional actions where we try to make the world and life more in line with our interests. These processes are taking place embedded in culture where our close relatives as parents support us by offering culturally organised understandings or meanings.

An important topic to create meaning of is our self. Other researchers have tried to describe the early understandings infants demonstrate (Spelke 1995) and some have described some of the sources by which an understanding of the self is created. As an example Stern (1985) talks about a 'core self' where the child realise that s/he

© The Author(s) 2019
K. Komatsu, *Meaning-Making for Living*, SpringerBriefs in Psychology,
https://doi.org/10.1007/978-3-030-19926-5

can act and influence the world and this demonstrates an able agent where the child's own actions can be distinguished from other peoples' actions.

Komatsu in this book take a different approach where he focuses on the processes through which infants and children create meaning and particularly how they develop an understanding of themselves in relation to their playmates in kindergarten or in school, their mother and others. By studying the micro-genetic processes in recorded dialogues or written diaries, he pinpoints the process and sees it as the child describing a grid of positions, relations and characteristics – that is an understanding of the social world the infant is part of. This grid is then used by the child to place her–/himself and by this showing and characterising who s/he her–/himself is as a person.

An important point for Komatsu is that this is ontologically understood not as an entity being more and more elaborated and/or revealed through life. Instead the self is conceptualised as dynamic and in a constant change and adjustment or confirmation whenever the person relates to her/his environment. The crucial point for Komatsu is then that the self is fluid and established in negotiation with others in relation to every episode. Development is the result of the tension between the understanding the child had before the present experience and the potentially new understanding of her–/himself presently revealed. With this ontological understanding of the self it is impossible to assess the self out of context since it is exactly in the way the child relates to and handles the context that the self appears. The self is not an entity existing across situations but rather an assembly of processes through which the child relates to the environment and her/his life. These processes are of course developed through life and qualified by culture and the child's own experiences. The processes are going on in a field of tension where the child has some interests in the outcome but the other parts in the current situation might also have interests in this whether these are present in a dialogue or imagined as when we write a text somebody else is going to read. There are then two kinds of tension:

- the tension the child experiences between her/his self-understanding to this moment and the present experience that might realise new aspects of the child's way of handling life – of the child's self
- the tension between different agents in the present situation who might have different interests in how the child should develop

This is how I understand Komatsu's ontological understanding of the concept of a self. When we then want to do research it is once again the processes that are of interest since the development of the person's self must be seen as a development of the processes by which the person relates to and acts in a situation. A mature person can be expected to relate to and act in a situation in a more sophisticated way incorporating more knowledge of the world and more competently act to further her/his own interests.

When we as researchers want to access these processes we should as Komatsu stresses study them in real-life situations or at least situations very close to real-life. If we arrange artificial situations as e.g. in most psychometric tests we will access the processes through which the person handles artificial situations which of course also is an aspect of the self. If our aim is to reveal something about how the person acts in everyday life then the test results can be quite misguiding.

Komatsu includes this as a crucial aspect of his theory by conceptualising it as the 'presentational self' – what he is investigating is the self as it is presented in situations – as it appears or shows in situations.

Self in a Cultural Frame

Uexküll (1934/2010) has developed an inspiring theory on how living species perceive their environment. Each species has developed a perceptual system attuned to the elements and aspects of normal living environments of that species but which might on the other hand ignore elements and aspects that are unimportant for their living. In this sense every individual only perceives an excerpt of the total environment and from this creates her/his own personal context. For humans I have tried to illustrate the processes in Fig. 1:

Fig. 1 A personal context

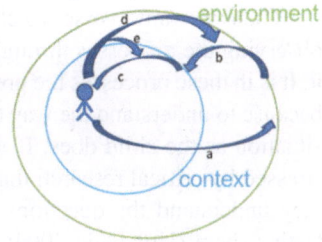

This figure illustrates the interplay between a person and the environment. The person acts on the environment and by this influences the development of the environment – arrow a. The person perceives the environment but no species perceive everything nor every aspect of the environment (Uexbüll 1934/2010). Different species are specialised through evolution in perceiving the parts and aspects of environment they need to survive but for humans part of this specialised perception is developed throughout life from experiences. Through childhood and the continued life we learn from experience and by this our perception is adjusted to fit what is important to handle our lives. Through this perceptual and developmental process we create our personal context from the specific experiences we have – arrow b. Since these are different from one person to another we in principle live in each our personal context that are more or less alike or different. Growing up in the same local community with a shared sub-culture we will however experience many of the same episodes and create relatively identical contexts and this raises no problems in daily interaction. Our experiences in our personal context influence our development of our self – arrow c.

As intentionally acting creatures we can decide to develop our context – arrow d – as we do when we decide to study a certain phenomenon in our environment. By this we deliberately change our personal context. As marked by arrow c our context influences us as persons but we are not passive creatures. We can to a certain degree decide how our environment should influence us – arrow e. As an example if somebody in our personal context keeps telling us, we are no good at sports we can decide not to let this influence our self-understanding nor our efforts. In fact we can decide to prove that s/he is wrong so it might have the opposite result.

In this figure the person is drawn in the centre of the circles but if we connect with Komatsu's text it should in fact be the assembly of the processes illustrated by the arrows that should be the self. In his empirical examples Komatsu especially illustrates the processes marked in the figure as arrow b and d. When the child enumerates friends in kindergarten and characterises them it is a process where experiences in the environment are analysed and ordered in the context of the child and ordering them in the context of the child implicitly characterises her–/himself in the same operation. In Komatsu's conceptualisation the child constructs a grid (personal context) in order to be able to place her/himself in relation to this. Komatsu mentions that he has not studied if and when the micro genetic processes actually result in a more enduring change of the ontological self.

When we want to assess a child we must – as learned from Komatsu – do this by observing the processes through which the child relates to the situation and handle it. It is in these processes the presentational self appears. Figure 1 adds another point because to understand the way the child handle the situation we have to perceive the situation as the child does. If we shortly return to standardised testing it has been stressed by critical research that when children fail at these tests it is often because they understand the questions and the situation differently than the psychologist testing them (Hundeide 2004; Säljö 2003). To perceive what a person is actually doing we have to understand how this particular person perceives the situation and this is not standardised but depending on the personal and constructed context. We have to take a first person perspective (Scraube 2015).

Bruner (1990) characterised children as incomplete at birth and the continuing development then takes place by experiences in the specific environment where the child grows up. As Fig. 1 illustrates this then results in the creation of different personal contexts and these contexts influence how a situation is perceived and understood. This is how the great variability (Valsiner 2014) among humans develops.

Komatsu's studies and theory show how the development and functioning of children and humans in general have to be studied by starting with the so called higher psychological functions since these guide and influence the simpler processes and this cannot be grasped the other way around. This does not imply that studies of the simpler processes are useless but they are organised by the person's attempts to handle life and are as such not autonomous.

Presentational Self in Applied Psychology

Resilience

The concept of resilience has since the start of the century become more commonly used within applied psychology whether this is educational psychology, psychotherapy or social work but simultaneously it has achieved quite different definitions and understandings. The concept originated in biology where it designated an ability to survive even challenging changes in the environment (Fitzpatrick 2011). Within developmental psychopathology it has developed to imply a complex and multilevel understanding where resilience is not a personal trait but a characteristic of the combined processes through which the person handles the challenges met in life and through which the environment influence the outcome – processes that include several levels as neurological, individual, social, societal processes (Cichetti 2010). It is important to be aware of the many different ways the concept of resilience is used, as there is no common accepted definition.

In Komatsu's theory we have the same focus on the dynamic processes as these unfold and on the individual as acting intentionally in her/his own life. Because Komatsu studies the micro genetic processes this might contribute to research in resilience since this is mainly done at the macro level with statistical correlations between conditions and individual characteristics. There is no doubt that resilience is enabled by the micro processes in everyday interaction so we need to study these to reveal the processes which we in the applied professions want to influence.

This connection of Komatsu's theory with resilience points to a need for developing the work with a focus on how the environment of the child interact with the child's processes of meaning making. How can different contributions of the mother influence the child's development of meaning making processes?

Drop Out of Students From Educations

Like in the case of resilience studies of students who drop out of education has developed from focusing on a personal trait to a more situational or contextual understanding. In the early understandings drop out was because the students were not clever enough where later additional aspects refer to characteristics such as lack of social competences or lack of cultural capital. These understandings still search for individual causes on the educational arena. Conceptualised by situational learning theory (Lave 1988, Lave and Wenger 1991) educational institutions plan for an institutional trajectory of participation (Nielsen 2008) where the students have a different perspective from their personal trajectory of participation and this include other arenas such as family, leisure activities, friends outside school among others.

If we analyse with Komatsu's theoretical frame, the individual student is constantly negotiating and creating a meaning with the episodes s/he experiences trying to establish an understanding of her/his self. If the different arenas include tensions that support different self-understandings or even undermine a self-understanding as a student – this could be family, old friends – then it can become too hard to maintain that identity (Nielsen 2016) and result in drop out. This is the second kind of fields of tension I mentioned above, but in all education the creation or development of the students' identity is implied at least to some degree (Packer and Goicoecha 2000) and this can create the first kind of tension. If the student experience a change that lead to separation from the social relations which have been important in her/his life until this moment then s/he will experience a tension between maintaining 'the old identity' versus changing to 'the new identity' as e.g. a craftsman (Hundeide 2005).

Processes in Therapeutic Settings

Psychodynamic traditions of psychotherapy understand the therapeutic process as using the therapeutic setting to develop and try out alternative ways of perceiving and acting (e.g. Horowitz 1989). This is an old tradition with a rich and detailed repertoire of concepts to describe and analyse these processes.

If we apply Komatsu's theory on these processes we have the same detailed focus on the micro genetic processes but the understanding of the self is even more processual. It would be interesting to use Komatsu's theoretical frame to analyse micro processes in psychotherapy. It does raise a problem though when Komatsu stresses that the self presents itself in relation to the specific situation and a psychotherapeutic setting is quite as artificial a situation as when we use psychometric testing. The client engages in an abnormal situation and is supposed to develop ways of perceiving and acting in everyday life. This is another way of posing the question of transfer (Tennant 1999) from the therapeutic setting to everyday life, which others have mentioned too (Dreier 2008). On the theoretical level it questions if there are processes of handling situations in ordinary life that can be observed even though the setting is artificial? Or to put it differently: how and when can observations in one setting be taken as indication of a pattern of acting in another setting?

Interesting Aspects to Investigate in the Future

Stability of Self

When we conceptualise the self as dynamic and as a process of constant negotiation, adjustment and confirmation then stability becomes a question of concern.

In fact I think everybody would agree that a self is constantly changing from one situation/context to the next situation/context and through time – looking back at our lives we can see the changes. Everybody would also agree that our self is more or less stable so we do not start from scratch every time we meet but recognise each other. The question is on which time scale we use for our observations. There is a tendency in occidental theories to conceptualise and verbalise every-thing (!) as entities and having trouble when we deal with processes (Bateson 1972). Here Komatsu's work help us by developing concepts to handle our self as processes. Considering the time scale a study of micro-genetic processes could lead to a focus on stability but Komatsu manages to demonstrate the processes even in micro genetic scale.

When we apply a process approach to our self, stability can be understood as the gradual achievement of a repertoire of perceptual and action procedures that manages many situations in everyday life. Our understanding of the environment and experiences in everyday life – our personal context as I described it above – becomes elaborated enough to handle most situations and since we do not meet many existential challenges we act in relatively stable ways. Stability is more a question of inertia since we do not change much. This is not the case for infants so Komatsu has chosen the right situations to develop his theory.

It would be interesting to develop the theory even further by focusing on when and why we change. When we perceive a situation we can find it well-known and as confirming our self understanding; or we could find it strange but un-important and not change; or we could find it puzzling and start elaborating on it and our self in it. This of course depends on earlier experiences or it might be seen as important by somebody so closely related to us that we prioritise it. Again the two kinds of tension are relevant to include. Here are different constellation among people.

Another topic in relation to stability is the balance between stability and change both presently and throughout life. In common sense it is often stated that you need a stable part of your life in order to manage challenges in the rest of everyday life. This is what attachment theory conceptualises as a need for a secure base in order to go out and investigate the world (Bowlby 1969). If you look at a life-perspective you have periods of much change and others characterised by greater stability. These balances would be interesting to investigate with the process approach Komatsu has developed.

Fields of Tension

Komatsu includes a concept of 'field of tension'. He studies microgenetic processes and describe how the child feels tension when reuniting after kindergarten and then work out a grid characterising the playmates in kindergarten in order to place her–/himself in relation to this. The process can also include negotiation of the relation between mother and child as to who know what about kindergarten. In these examples the tension is mainly a tension for the child who has had some experiences that create a demand for re-establishing her/his self. Komatsu points to the need for further research on when these microgenetic processes result in a more stable change in the child's self.

I feel tempted to expand the concept of fields of tension as I did above and have done earlier on (Jensen 2018). My main research field is youths in social care because of social or personal problems. If you look at the situation for most of these youths, there are many persons who have an opinion on who they are and who they should be. Work in this field is often dominated by some looking back at their life until now and expecting a self that continues her/his actions because the self is seen as rather stable. On the other hand especially adolescence is often described as a period where youths are seeking for an identity and trying out different roles. Common is an effort to teach moral and responsibility as a personal characteristic expecting that this can guide their actions in a more suitable direction. This understanding sees the problem as localised in the person. In other cases some of these youths are characterised as field-dependent: they are not able to take their own standpoint but adjust to the company they are in. Again the challenge is seen as developing a personality that acts as responsible for her/his own actions. An understanding focusing on internal personality characteristics.

If we analyse the challenges of this kind of social work with the concept of a presentational self the focus becomes different. Adolescence can be described (at least as it is understood in occidental cultures) as a period where youths are unsure of their own self and willing to try out suggestions. Everybody is negotiating and creating meaning but adolescents are more open than people later in life are. Then this is not a question of an intrapsychic characteristic but a way of handling a process of creating meaning of the situation including positioning oneself. To assess the challenge in social work becomes a question of developing ability to handle processes of self-maintenance in a field of tension where different persons and groups have their interests in the outcome of these processes. It is not only a question of intrapsychic moral standpoints but a competence to handle processes of self development in different fields of tension and for some a greater focus on these processes could be more beneficial.

How to Research on Presentational Self

Komatsu makes a clear distinction between the self in an ontological sense and our epistemological efforts to perceive and describe the self. As described the self in an ontological sense is conceptualised as the relative stable characteristics of the way the person handle his/her life. In an epistemological sense, the self shows or presents itself in relation to specific episodes and the processes of handling this specific episode can give us the opportunity to observe the self in action – in process. You could argue that everyday episodes involve questions just like assessment instruments so the researcher could assess the child using these instruments. This might be true for research but for practitioners they need to assess the child in relation to fields of tension in their everyday life since it is in these connections their efforts should be useful.

Komatsu studies episodes of re-union – episodes where infants and mothers see each other again after a day in kindergarten. He mentions that these episodes have special potentiality because they lay ground for a negotiation of sameness – non-sameness – how is the child the same and what could be added or changed in the understanding of the self?

Another aspect of a day in kindergarten is the fact that it is a part of the child's life that is invisible for the mother so a re-union include handling the question of visible – in-visible too.

An interesting point that Komatsu does not address is the question of how great a need for negotiation is at play in these situations. When the child is in kindergarten this establish a part of her/his life that is invisible for the mother and the child might have changed during this period. In that case a reunion bring forth a need for negotiation because of these (for the mother) invisible episodes. If we try to generalise this a bit you could see situations that in one way or another question your self and your position could potentially be episodes for studying the presentational self. Other examples of potentially productive episodes could be when somebody question your self perception by characterising you differently than you would do, or episodes where you are placed in a new environment with new interests or where well-known situations suddenly change concerning interests and by this changes the field of tension. The list can be continued but the idea is to search for situations where established self understanding is challenged since we can expect that this will prompt processes of meaning making and by this show the presentational self.

Exactly here we might expect differences depending on who challenges your self understanding. If this is done by somebody who is of great importance to you then the processes might be prompted easier and quicker. Likewise if the episode concerns aspects of your self that you see as core characteristics of your self. The dynamics of the connection between processes of meaning making and personal relations and/or important values and personal investment would be interesting to research further.

When two people meet and interact the process will always include negotiation of their identity/selves and their relation to each other (Hundeide 2004) but for people who have known each other for a long time this will be rather subtle. On the contrary, if one or both of them have experienced something that really impressed them on an existential level then we can expect the processes of meaning making and creating an understanding of oneself will be more dominant. This could be a separation as when the child has been in kindergarten but it could also be after experiences of accidents, after giving birth, overcoming hardship, passing milestones in life, losing your parents etc. Experiences that are so marked that your self-understanding might be questioned.

It is important to notice that whether this is the case cannot be established objectively but it depends on the experience of the person. Again a cultural psychological point: the importance of an experience depends on the person experiencing and cannot be standardised.

This also imply that some situations can be judged as non-exceptional and so usual that the person does not need to spend resources on creating new meaning and understanding of the self.

Another consideration in selecting situations where you can expect the processes of meaning making and presentational self to appear is the participating persons. Even if an episode has been very special then the person will presumably prefer to consider the influence on her/his self with persons whom s/he knows and rely upon. Even a very impressive episode might result in little opportunity of observing self maintenance processes if you have to discuss with an unknown researcher. Then these processes will be postponed until you have opportunity to discuss with a related person as with your mother on the way home from kindergarten. Again this does not mean that if only a related person is part of the dialogue then these self maintenance processes will appear. Exactly being together with well-known people diminishes the need for renegotiation of your self so if nothing has left you with unresolved problems these processes could be very hard to perceive in such interaction.

Komatsu includes the researcher in his models describing the processes where the presentational self appears – see Fig. 2 as example. When the researcher analyses the recordings of a dialogue between a mother and a child the researcher might end up with different understandings on what is going on. To validate these understandings you have to return to the episode and the environment in which the dialogue took place. This is clearly in line with Komatsu's theory: you cannot omit the environment since this is the field of tension in which the child has to manoeuvre and if we want to understand the processes by which the child creates meaning then we have to include the environment with it's specific challenges and constraints for meaning creation.

Likewise validation of interpretations has to return to the specific situation in order to clarify different results. We do not have direct access to the experiences of another person related to the personal context so the closest we can get is through observing and understanding the present environment, the processes through which the person perceives including her/his personal context and her/his meaning. The last two aspects we only access by observing and listening and then identify with the processes to follow them.

Closing Remarks

I think the most important contribution Komatsu brings us with this text is his consistent development of concepts and methods to study the processes of human meaning creation as this is taking place at a micro-genetic level in everyday life. This statement of 'human as meaning creating' sometimes becomes a little shallow but in Komatsu's analysis he demonstrates – sometimes just in passing – how this has consequences for our understanding of the self and our methods for doing research on this. I see great potentials in continuing theory development and research along these lines.

About the Author

Mogens Jensen is associate professor in 'educational psychology in social work' at the Department of Communication and Psychology, Aalborg University, Denmark. He has worked and done research within social-pedagogical treatment with vulnerable youths and with qualifying the pedagogues who work in this field.

References

Bateson, G. (1972). *Steps to an ecology of mind.* New York: Ballantine Books.

Bowlby, J. (1969). *Attachment and Loss.* London: Hogarth Press.

Bruner, J. (1990). *Acts of meaning.* Cambridge Mass.: Harvard University Press.

Cichetti, D. (2010). 'Resilience under conditions of extreme stress: a multilevel perspective' in *World Psychiatry.* 9:145–154.

Dreier, O. (2008). *Psychotherapy in everyday life.* Cambridge: Cambridge University Press.

Fitzpattrick, C. (2011). 'What is the Difference between 'Desistance' and 'Resilience'? Exploring the Relationship between Two Key Concepts' in *Youth Justice,* 11(3), 221–234.

Horowitz, M. (1989). *Introduction to psychodynamics.* London: Routledge.

Hundeide, K. (2004). *Børns livsverden og sociokulturelle rammer [Children's lifeworld and socio-cultural frames].* København: Akademisk Forlag.

Hundeide, K. (2005). 'Socio-cultural tracks of development, opportunity structures and access skills' in *Culture and Psychology,* 11(2), 241–261.

Jensen, M. (2018). 'Emergence of self situated at an institution' in *Emergence of self in educational contexts* Springer Nature.

Lave, J. (1988). *Cognition in practice.* Cambridge: Cambridge University Press.

Lave, J. & Wenger, L. (1991). *Situated learning: legitimate peripheral participation.* Cambridge: Cambridge University Press.

Nielsen, K. (2008). 'Learning, trajectories of participation and social practice' in *Critical Social Studies* 1 22–36.

Nielsen, K. (2016). 'Engagement, conduct of life and dropouts in the Danish vocational education and training (VET) system' in *Journal of Vocational Education and Training* 68(2), 198–213.

Packer, I. & Goicoecha, (2000). 'Sociocultural and constructivist theories of learning: Ontology, not just epistemology'. *Educational Psychologist, 35*(4), 227–241.

Schraube, E. (2015). 'Why theory matters: Analytical strategies of critical psychology' in *Estudos de Psicologia,* Vol. 32(3) p. 533–545.

Spelke, E. (1995). 'Initial knowledge: six suggestions'. In J. Mehler & S. Franck (Eds.) *Cognition on cognition* Amsterdam: Elsevier Science Publishers p. 433–447.

Stern, D. (1985). *The interpersonal world of the infant.* London: Routledge.

Säljö, R. (2003). *Læring i praksis: et sociokulturelt perspektiv [Learning in practice: a sociocultural perspective]* København: Hans Reitzels Forlag.

Tennant, M. (1999). 'Is learning transferable?' in D. Boud (Ed.) *Understanding learning at work.* London: Routledge 165–179.

Uexküll, J. V. (1934/2010). *A foray into the worlds of animals and humans.* Minneapolis: University of Minnesota Press.

Valsiner, J. (2007). *Culture in minds and societies.* London: Sage.

Valsiner, J. (2014). *An invitation to cultural psychology.* London: Sage.

Valsiner, J., Marsico, G., Chaudhary, N., Sato, T. & Dazzani, V. (Eds.) (2016). *Psychology as the Science of Human.* Being/Heidelberg: Springer.

Commentary 2
Children Emerging Laughingly Through Dialogue

Tania Zittoun

In *Meaning-making for living*, Koji Komatsu invites us to accompany him discretely in improbable places: in the car of Japanese mothers bringing their children to and from schools, and in the school diaries of small Japanese children at school. These moments and places are surprising and poetic, as when a little girl laughingly discusses whether she is a snow, moon or flower-rabbit with her playful driving mother. Looking at these dialogues, Koji Komatsu does a series of audacious methodological and theoretical moves. I propose to discuss them further, bringing in the dialogue studies within sociocultural, dialogical and developmental psychology that share some of the qualitative, process-oriented assumptions chosen by the author.

Studying the Development of Children

The first series of interesting moves proposed by Koji Komatsu are methodological, and with it, epistemological. Development involves the change of a specific person, in *time*. As tautological as it seems, it is actually difficult to document change. In his little book, Komatsu presents the result of years of work around two sets of data that reflect two of the main ways to study ontogenesis: in real-time recorded data, and in longitudinal self-writings.

First, development is studied through actual longitudinal data, documenting the life of two children, through time. Komatsu constituted this rich corpus of about 100 hours of mother-child daily dialogues, recorded by the mother at the demand of the (absent) researcher. These data have thus the freshness and beauty of these stolen moments, while be highly informative of the development of young children (between 4 and 5, for the girl (Mina) and between 5 and 6 for the boy (Yuuma)). Although there is a growth of large cohort longitudinal studies with children (e.g., Weller 2012), there are not so many of these longitudinal case-studies, but all are highly informative. One of these is for instance the paradigmatic case of the little

© The Author(s) 2019   129
K. Komatsu, *Meaning-Making for Living*, SpringerBriefs in Psychology,
https://doi.org/10.1007/978-3-030-19926-5

Emily recorded in her auto-dialogues, and studied by many authors since (Nelson 2006). In addition, Komatsu uses here a mobile method – studying children in a car trip; if it has been already used to explore children's perspective (Barker 2009; Ross et al. 2009), the originality here is to use it longitudinally.

Second, Komatsu studied longitudinal self-writing, by studying children's diaries; here, the Japanese school and its cultivation of the singularity of the child and its expression through *nikki*, diary writing, create interesting conditions to observe children's daily addressed reflection upon their evolving daily experiences. Although the author prefers to analyse micro-genetic movements – what happens in one entry of a child's *nikki* – the data offers the potential to follow the same child over time, and to observe how the writing evolves, also participating and reflecting transformations of the person (Gillespie and Zittoun 2010; Zittoun and Gillespie 2012).

As stated earlier, development involves the change of a *specific person*, in time. Again, as tautological as it may appear, it is not so current that developmental study focus on the development of a given person. Studies classically have examined the development of a function, or a skill (hence, Piaget's children have been studied as cases of the development of cognition of representations (Piaget 2000)), Emily has been studied as case of the development of language, etc.). There is however a thin thread of studies that consider seriously the child as a person, and that person's perspective upon the world (Hedegaard et al. 2012). For instance, Pernille Hviid has accounted, through ethnographic observations, for the development of a young boy's engagement, in and out of school, and the strategies he deployed to maintain what was important for him, as a person, against the demands of the teachers (Hviid 2015). Such accounts require an epistemological move, where the researcher has to renounce some of his or her omnipotence, and to try to approach, as much as possible, the child's first person perspective. Of course, it is difficult, as the researcher is always in a third person perspective; but here, by bringing both naturalistic mother-child dialogues and first-person writings in dialogue. Koji Komatsu creates the condition for a study of a first-person perspective.

Finally, development involves the *change* of *a specific person,* in time. Development is obviously about change, but change is at times difficult to capture as days go by and resemble each other. In effect, in the daily adjustments to the new colours in the sky, the new cars met in the street, new exercises at school, a lot seems quite regular, and feels more like repetition with variation than actually change. Here, the coup of Komatsu resides in focusing on moments where changes takes place a bit more, in what he calls "transitions" and at times "liminal spaces". In effect, data is collected during the trip to and back from school, or through diaries that report daily life in the school. These places and times, the trip or the diary-writing, have thus a status of in-between, or rather, of moving from one type of experience, located in one setting, to another one. These in that sense escape the structures of these settings, and the position the child has within; not anymore there, the child is not yet elsewhere. These liminal experiences are per definition more fluid and potentially transformative (Stenner 2018), and offer thus ideal points of entry to study the emergence of the self and more generally development.

Theorising the Development of Children

Koji Komatsu's main argument is that children's self is not a stable entity or an essence, but rather, that self emerges through dynamic processes of sharing and differentiation; eventually, in dialogical dynamics, the self is presentational. Hence, for example, Mina's self precisely emerges as she presents herself as a moon rabbit, to be distinguished from snow and flower rabbits, within the dialogue she has with her mother, also referring to dialogical dynamics that took place at school. To build his argument, Komatsu develops a semiotic cultural theoretical framework, where the heart of sense-making has to be found in A – non-A dynamics (Josephs 1998; Josephs and Valsiner 1998; Valsiner 2007), which actually correspond to the definition and slow evolution of what he calls "meaning complexes". These meaning complexes indeed strongly recall Vygotsky's pseudo-concepts (Vygotsky 1986), the child constitution of meaningful, affect-laden assemblages of relational, embodied, active experiences, which take their contour precisely through games of variation, permutation and contrast. Note however how playful and alive are these moments – far from theoretical conceptual exercises, they precisely take place in vital parent-child emotionally charged interactions, within the history of their relation (Hinde et al. 1985).

Komatsu also highlights that these presentational dynamics take place so as to enable the participants to present who they are to the other – what they do, feel and experience – outside of the relationship. Mothers learn about the person that is their child through daily discussion about school, and teachers discover the person that is their student through diary referring to experiences out of school. In that sense, the discussion-about-the-school-day or the child's diary (*nikki*) can be seen as cultural artefacts that both mediate two worlds – two aspects of the world of the child, for an adult – and artefacts that transform the child. In effect, by telling her mother about her day at school, the now-independent child recreates the relation she has with her mother; by writing about zoo visits, the child at school learns to wave that experience within his or her school experiences as student. In that sense, these cultural artefacts – the genre of discussion-about-the-school-day or the *nikki* entry – can be seen as liminal affective technologies (Stenner 2018; Stenner and Moreno-Gabriel 2013): they are semiotic dispositives participating to the development of the child.

Koji Komatsu proposes to analyse these transformative moments as dialectical dynamics between same-non-same, and visible-invisible. In effect, these dialogues enable to make visible to the other what he or she doesn't see, and take place through dynamics of resemblance and differentiation. If this analysis has the quality of simplicity, and allows the author to bring interesting variations of the role of repetition and variation in music, and the evolution of invisibility in the history of religions, I however believe that there is room for alternative and more integrative solutions.

From a lifecourse perspective, it may be said that children aged 4 or 5, as Mina or Yuuma, are exploring new spaces and settings out of home, their "first socialisation" environment, and are creating new spheres of experiences, within the setting of the classroom (Zittoun et al. 2013). Spheres of experiences are configurations of lived experiences, involving certain activities, relationship, modes of being, range of skills, which are recurrent enough for a given person to be recognized as "the same"; the concept designates a reality partly phenomenologically experienced, partly defined by the social and material environment (Zittoun and Gillespie 2016). Children discovering school are creating new spheres of experiences, that of exercise with the teacher and the class, of lunch-with-one's-group, of diary-writing, etc. One may thus say that children and their mother talking about the school days are, first, establishing and renewing, each of them, a sphere of experience of being-with-the other, within the mother-child relationship. A mother-child close interaction thus involves overlapping spheres of experience – the sphere-of-being with the other, which is obviously different for the mother than for the child (Zittoun et al. 2018). The experience of overlapping spheres functions as long as mother and child maintain a shared inter-subjectivity, feel that they are attuned (Trevarthen 2012). However, the child has engaged new spheres of experience, and as Komatsu shows, the mother who wants to know about the invisible-to-her experience of her child has to ask her about these. In other words, the mother convokes, in the present overlapping proximal sphere experience, another sphere of experience of the child, to which she never can direct access. The child, through the mediation of language and within the warm interaction with the mother, learns to convoke, construct and re-present what was lived earlier: she creates a distal sphere of experience – based on traces and memories of her formerly present sphere of experience, when still at school. Doing so, the child thus accomplishes two things: first, she participates to the nourishment of the overlapping spheres of experiences with the mother; second, she also learns, through externalisation via language and probably non-linguistic modes (giggles, moves, etc.), through semiotic elaboration, to transform her formerly lived experience in a semiotised and social one (Nelson 1996, 2001; Valsiner 2000, 2007). Once semiotised as distal experiences, these spheres of experience get some stability; the child can return to them through imagination. In that ways, the child slowly starts to expand her configuration of spheres of experience: she is not only what she is in the here-and-now, but also, she is what she can experience through distancing, and exploring past and soon future experience – through her imaginary movement through symbolic spaces (distal experiences). Hence, the child explores with the mother the dialogicality of herself, across the configuration of her proximal and distal experiences.

To add one level of complication, we can also recall that two of the most emblematic excerpts reported by Koji Komatsu, the moon rabbit scene (1.2) and the maze play (3.2) are actually narration from the child about playing or fictional experiences. Although this is not addressed explicitly by the author, it is worth mentioning, as the importance of play and fiction is primordial in children development. Children aged 4–5 play easily, and in principle, know when they act in the socially shared reality where things are as they are, or in a play-world, where a child can be a bunny, and they learn to master the subtle cue to enter or move out of a world-play (e.g., "now let's say I were a tiger" or "I don't play anymore"), that is, to create the boundary of a distal sphere of experience (Harris 2000; Hviid and Villadsen 2018;

Singer and Singer 1992; Winnicott 2001). In each of Komatsu's sequences, the child reports about past spheres of experience, during which he or she was defining the modalities and the conditions of creating *another* distal, playing, sphere of experience. They also report engaging in that distal sphere of experiences were they met their friends-as-rabbits: suddenly the reality of the school was overridden by a complex world of rabbits-meeting. In that respect, the mother-child dialogue is the frame, within which the proximal experience of talking-with-mother takes place, and where he or she convokes a distal experience, which was itself a distal experience in relation to the actual reality of school; it is thus an attempt to create a "squared" distal sphere of experience. Following such reasoning, I may suggest that the mother-child interaction constitutes a sphere of proximal experience for the child, in which she learns to navigate to, through and from distal spheres of experiences – both in the sense of past and fictional. This, we may say, is possible through the kind guidance of the adult's hints, reactions and reformulation, as well as emotional tuning, which both validate the distal experience of the child and supports its maintenance. In that sense, the mother-child daily interaction may be an important place to anchor and learn to use imagination as expansion of experience – learning to navigate through real and possible worlds.

Such reading also supports the claim that these dialogues are locus of emergence of the self: if Komatsu is right that identity is not an essence, children (and we) still need to experience being still-the-same (Erikson 1968; Hviid 2012), a sense of continuity achieved only through the capacity to navigate across proximal and distal experiences, and establishing some forms of semiotic links across these, some modalities of integration (Zittoun and Gillespie 2015). Thus, finally, Koji Komatsu may have shown one more of the many vital functions of child-parent interactions, that of accompanying the child through his movement through proximal and distal spheres of experiences, through geographical and symbolic spaces, and developing modalities of integrating these.

For Further Development

In this short commentary, I have tried to bring to the fore two of the main contributions of Koji Komatsu's original little book on the emergence of the presentational self. On the one hand, I have emphasised the relevance of his methodological proposition: collecting longitudinal data, both recorded in absence, and produced via self-writings, in potentially transformative moments – or at least, in moments calling for the integration of diverse experiences -, and also potentially enabling to combine first and third person analysis. On the other hand, I have tried to summarize the original theoretical proposition of Koji Komatsu: liminal moments such as diary-writing and mother-child conversation in trips from schools are the locus of the emergence of a presentational self, dialectically constructing through meaning-making, via tensions between the visible and the invisible, the same and the non-same. I have attempted to push this reasoning one step further by linking it with recent analysis in lifecourse development, and suggested that these shared interactions may also be seen as moments in which an adult accompanies and supports the child in his or her exploration and binding of proximal and distal spheres of experiences, supporting the child imagination as expansion of experience. Along these two lines, Koji Komatsu invites many further dialogues and towards generalisation and theoretical integration.

About the Author

Tania Zittoun develops a sociocultural psychology of the lifecourse, with a specific focus on the dynamics of imagination. Her theoretical work is in dialogue with psychoanalysis and the critical social sciences. She currently studies regional case studies to address issues related to mobility and ageing. She is Associate Editor of Culture & Psychology, and her last books are Imagination in Human and Cultural development (with Alex Gillespie, Routledge, 2016) and the Handbook of culture and imagination (OUP, 2018, co-edited with Vlad P. Glaveanu).

References

Barker, D. J. (2009). 'Driven to distraction?': Children's experiences of car travel. *Mobilities*, 4(1), 59–76. https://doi.org/10.1080/17450100802657962

Erikson, E. H. (1968). *Identity: youth and crisis*. London: Faber & Faber.

Gillespie, A., & Zittoun, T. (2010). Studying the movement of thought. In A. Toomela & J. Valsiner (Eds.), *Methodological thinking in psychology: 60 years gone astray?* (pp. 69–88). Charlotte, NC: Information Age Publisher.

Harris, P. L. (2000). *The work of the imagination* (1st ed.). Oxford/Malden, MA: Wiley-Blackwell.

Hedegaard, M., Aronsson, K., & Hojholt, C. (2012). *Children, childhood, and everyday life: Children's perspectives*. IAP.

Hinde, R. A., Perret-Clermont, A. N., & Hinde, J. S. (1985). *Social relationships and cognitive development*. Oxford: Clarendon Press.

Hviid, P. (2012). "Remaining the same" and children's experience of development. In M. Hedegaard, K. Aronsson, C. Hojholt, & O. Ulvik (Eds.), *Children, childhood, and everyday life: Children's perspectives* (pp. 37–52). Charlotte: Information Age Publishing, Inc.

Hviid, P. (2015). Borders in education and living– a case of trench warfare. *Integrative Psychological and Behavioral Science*, 50(1), 44–61. https://doi.org/10.1007/s12124-015-9319-1

Hviid, P., & Villadsen, J. W. (2018). Playing and being – imagination in the life course. In T. Zittoun & V. P. Glăveanu (Eds.), *Handbook of culture and imagination* (pp. 137–166). Oxford/New York: Oxford University Press.

Josephs, I. E. (1998). Constructing one's self in the city of the silent: Dialogue, symbols, and the role of "as-if" in self-development. *Human Development*, 41(3), 180–195.

Josephs, I. E., & Valsiner, J. (1998). How does autodialogue work? Miracles of meaning maintenance and circumvention strategies. *Social Psychology Quarterly*, 61(1), 68–83.

Nelson, K. (1996). *Language in cognitive development. Emergence of the mediated mind*. Cambridge: Cambridge University Press.

Nelson, K. (2001). Language and the self: From the "Experiencing I" to the "Continuing Me." In *The self in time: Developmental perspectives* (pp. 15–33). Mahwah, NJ, US: Lawrence Erlbaum Associates Publishers.

Nelson, K. (Ed.). (2006). *Narratives from the crib* (2nd, oringal publication 1989 ed.). Cambridge, MA: Harvard University Press.

Piaget, J. (2000). *The Construction of reality in the child* (Original 1937). London: Routledge.

Ross, N. J., Renold, E., Holland, S., & Hillman, A. (2009). Moving stories: using mobile methods to explore the everyday lives of young people in public care. *Qualitative Research, 9*(5), 605–623. https://doi.org/10.1177/1468794109343629

Singer, D. G., & Singer, J. L. (1992). *The house of make-believe: Children's play and the developing imagination* (Reprint). Cambridge, MA: Harvard University Press.

Stenner, P. (2018). *Liminality and experience. A transdisciplinary approach to the psychosocial.* London: Palgrave Macmillan.

Stenner, P., & Moreno-Gabriel, E. (2013). Liminality and affectivity: The case of deceased organ donation. *Subjectivity, 6*(3), 229–253. https://doi.org/10.1057/sub.2013.9

Trevarthen, C. (2012). Embodied human intersubjectivity: Imaginative agency, to share meaning. *Cognitive Semiotics, 4*(1), 6–56.

Valsiner, J. (2000). *Culture and human development.* Thousand Oaks: Sage.

Valsiner, J. (2007). *Culture in minds and societies: Foundations of cultural psychology.* New Delhi: Sage.

Vygotsky, L. S. (1986). *Thought and Language.* (A. Kozulin, Ed.) (Revised). Cambridge, MA: The MIT Press.

Weller, S. (2012). Evolving creativity in qualitative longitudinal research with children and teenagers. *International Journal of Social Research Methodology: Theory & Practice, 15*(2), 119–133. https://doi.org/10.1080/13645579.2012.649412

Winnicott, D. W. (2001). *Playing and reality.* Philadelphia/Sussex: Routledge.

Zittoun, T., & Gillespie, A. (2012). Using diaries and self-writings as data in psychological research. In E. Abbey & S. E. Surgan (Eds.), *Emerging Methods in Psychology* (pp. 1–26). New Brunswick, NJ/London, UK: Transaction Publishers.

Zittoun, T., & Gillespie, A. (2015). Integrating experiences: Body and mind moving between contexts. In B. Wagoner, N. Chaudhary, & P. Hviid (Eds.), *Integrating experiences: Body and mind moving between contexts* (pp. 3–49). Charlotte: Information Age Publishing.

Zittoun, T., & Gillespie, A. (2016). *Imagination in human and cultural development.* London: Routledge.

Zittoun, T., Levitan, D., & Cangiá, F. (2018). A sociocultural approach to mobile families: A case study. *Peace and Conflict: Journal of Peace Psychology, 24*(4), 424–432.

Zittoun, T., Valsiner, J., Vedeler, D., Salgado, J., Gonçalves, M., & Ferring, D. (2013). *Human development in the lifecourse. Melodies of living.* Cambridge: Cambridge University Press.

References

Ainsworth, M. D. S., Blehar, M. C., Waters, E., & Wall, S. (1978). *Patterns of attachment: A psychological study of the strange situation*. Hillsdale, NJ: Lawrence Erlbaum.

Aukrust, V. G. (2002). "What did you do in school today?" Speech genres and tellability in multiparty family mealtime conversations in two cultures. In S. Blum-Kulka & C. E. Snow (Eds.), *Talking to adults: The contribution of multiparty discourse to language acquisition* (pp. 55–83). Mahwah, NJ: Lawrence Erlbaum.

Baldwin, J. M. (1892). Origin of volition in childhood. *Science, 20*(511), 286–287.

Bamberg, M. (2011). Who am I? Narration and its contribution to self and identity. *Theory and Psychology, 21*(1), 3–24.

Blum-Kulka, S. (1997). *Dinner talk: Cultural patterns of sociability and socialization in family discourse*. Mahwah, NJ: Lawrence Erlbaum.

Blum-Kulka, S. (2002). "Do you believe that Lot's wife is blocking the road (to Jericho)?": Co-constructing theories about the world with adults. In S. Blum-Kulka & C. E. Snow (Eds.), *Talking to adults: The contribution of multiparty discourse to language acquisition* (pp. 85–115). Mahwah, NJ: Lawrence Erlbaum.

Bradbard, M. R., Endsley, R. C., & Mize, J. (1992). The ecology of parent-child communications about daily experiences in preschool and day care. *Journal of Research in Childhood Edcation, 6*(2), 131–141.

Damon, W., & Hart, D. (1988). *Self-understanding in childhood and adolescence*. New York: Cambridge University Press.

Dubois, S., & Sankoff, D. (2001). The variationist approach toward discourse structural effects and socio-interactional dynamics. In D. Schiffrin, D. Tannen, & H. E. Hamilton (Eds.), *The handbook of discourse analysis* (pp. 282–303). Oxford: Blackwell.

Ferreiro, E. (1985). The interplay between information and assimilation in beginning literacy. In W. H. Teale & E. Sulzby (Eds.), *Emergent literacy: Writing and Reading* (pp. 15–49). Norwood, NJ: Ablex.

Fivush, R., Haden, C. A., & Reese, E. (2006). Elaborating on elaborations: Role of maternal reminiscing style in cognitive and socioemotional development. *Child Development, 77*(6), 1568–1588.

Funabashi, K. (1996). A study on the 'Seikatsu-tsuzurikata' practice by Ichitaro Kokubun: On his practice and discourse in the movement of 'Hoppou-sei' education. *Annual report of the Department of Education, Rikkyo University, 39*, 87–99. (in Japanese).

© The Author(s) 2019
K. Komatsu, *Meaning-Making for Living*, SpringerBriefs in Psychology,
https://doi.org/10.1007/978-3-030-19926-5

Georgakopoulou, A. (2002). Greek children and familiar narratives in family contexts: En route to cultural performances. In S. Blum-Kulka & C. E. Snow (Eds.), *Talking to adults: The contribution of multiparty discourse to language acquisition* (pp. 33–54). Mahwah, NJ: Lawrence Erlbaum.

Giesen, B. (2012). Iconic difference and seduction. In J. C. Alexander, D. Bartmański, & B. Giesen (Eds.), *Iconic power: Materiality and meaning in social life* (pp. 203–218). New York: Palgrave Macmillan.

Gillespie, A. (2007). The social basis of self-reflection. In J. Valsiner & A. Rosa (Eds.), *The Cambridge handbook of sociocultural psychology* (pp. 678–691). New York: Cambridge University Press.

Griffiths, P. (1981). *Cage (Oxford studies of composers 18)*. London: Oxford University Press.

Griffiths, P. (2006). *A concise history of western music*. New York: Cambridge University Press.

Haden, C. A., Haine, R. A., & Fivush, R. (1997). Developing narrative structure in parent-child reminiscing across the preschool years. *Developmental Psychology, 33*(2), 295–307.

Harré, R., & van Langenhove, L. (1999). The dynamics of social episodes. In R. Harré & L. van Langenhove (Eds.), *Positioning theory: Moral contexts of intentional action* (pp. 1–13). Malden: Blackwell.

Harter, S. (1999). *The construction of the self: A developmental perspective*. New York: Guilford.

Hatano, I. (1932). 児童の夢の絵(一) 形態的研究 (Paintings of dreams by children I: A study of their forms). *Japanese Journal of. Psychology, 7*(1), 67–101. (in Japanese).

Heath, S. B. (1983). *Ways with words: Language, life, and work in communities and classrooms*. New York: Cambridge University Press.

Hinds, J. (1986). *Situation vs. person focus*. Tokyo: Kuroshio Shuppan.

Hiraoka, S. (2011). The ideology and practices of "Seikatsu-Tsuzurikata": Education by teaching of expressive writing. *Educational Studies in Japan: International Yearbook, 6*, 21–31.

Iida, K. (2013). A study of events connected with Seikatsu Tsuzurikata Kyouiku ("Composition based on daily life"): The concept of "Self" in Zuiisendai ("Free selection of a theme on writing education") by Ashida Enosuke. *Gakko Kyoikugaku Kenkyu Kiyo, University of Tsukuba, 6*, 55–73. (in Japanese).

Innis, R. E. (2009). *Susanne Langer in focus: The symbolic mind*. Bloomington, IN: Indiana University Press.

James, W. (1890). *The principles of psychology*. New York: Henry Holt.

Jonckheere, K. (2012). *Antwerp art after iconoclasm: Experiments in decorum 1566–1585*. Brussels: Mercatorfonds.

Josephs, I. E., Valsiner, J., & Surgan, S. E. (1999). The process of meaning construction: Dissecting the flow of semiotic activity. In J. Brandtstädter & R. M. Lerner (Eds.), *Action and self-development: Theory and research through the life span* (pp. 257–282). Thousand Oaks, CA: Sage.

Kajii, Y. (2001). How do teachers evaluate elementary school children's compositions? Validity and teachers' use of criteria. *Japanese Journal of Educational Psychology, 49*(4), 480–490. (in Japanese).

Katz, D., & Katz, R. (1936). *Conversations with children*. London: Kegan Paul, Trench, Trubner & Co.

Komatsu, K. (2000). Co-narrating about children's experiences at preschool: Mothers' beliefs about and perceptions of their conversations with their children. *Japanese Journal of Educational Psychology, 48*(4), 481–491. (in Japanese).

Komatsu, K. (2002). 「経験を語る」ことと子どもの自己 (Children's talk about past experiences and the self). In T. Mori (Ed.), 認知心理学者新しい学びを語る *(Discussing education through cognitive psychology)* (pp. 100–111). Kyoto: Kitaoji Shobo. (in Japanese).

Komatsu, K. (2003). Mother-child conversations about kindergarten friends, teachers and experiences: Conversation topics and the characteristics of children's speech. *Japanese Journal of Developmental Psychology, 14*(3), 294–303. (in Japanese).

Komatsu, K. (2006). The construction of a young child's self in mother-child conversations: A longitudinal case study focusing on "the self in relation to others". *Japanese Journal of Developmental Psychology, 17*(2), 115–125. (in Japanese).

Komatsu, K. (2010). Emergence of young children's presentational self in daily conversation and its semiotic foundation. *Human Development, 53*(4), 208–228.

Komatsu, K. (2012). Temporal reticence of the self: Who can know my self? *Integrative Psychological and Behavioral Science, 46*(3), 357–372.

Komatsu, K. (2013). Why and how young children's presentational self emerges in day-to-day conversation about the past? Focusing on children's daily trip to yochien, in Japan. In G. Marsico, K. Komatsu, & A. Iannaccone (Eds.), *Crossing boundaries: Intercontextual dynamics between family and school* (pp.109–133). Charlotte, NC: Information Age.

Komatsu, K. (2015). Otherness is everywhere to bring about your self: An inquiry into the whimsical emergence of children's selves. In J. Valsiner, G. Marsico, N. Chaudhary, T. Sato, & V. Dazzani (Eds.), *Psychology as the science of human being: The Yokohama manifesto* (pp. 287–297). Cham: Springer International.

Komatsu, K. (2016). On the dialectic nature of human mind: The dynamic tension between sameness and non-sameness. *Integrative Psychological and Behavioral Science, 50*(1), 174–183.

Komatsu, K. (2017). Not seeing is believing: The role of invisibility in human lives. *Integrative Psychological and Behavioral Science, 51*(1), 14–28.

Komatsu, K., & Konno, C. (2014). Children's presentational self in their personal stories: An exploration of third-grade students' writings from a semiotic perspective. *Japanese Journal of Developmental Psychology, 25*(3), 323–335. (in Japanese).

Komatsu, K., & Noguchi, T. (2001). Significance and function of mother-child conversations about children's daily experiences at kindergarten. *Memoirs of Osaka Kyoiku University (Ser. 4), 50*(1), 61–78. (in Japanese).

Langer, S. K. (1948). *Philosophy in a new key: A study in the symbolism of reason, rite, and art.* New York: New American Library.

Levine, P. (2007). Sharing common ground: The role of place reference in parent-child conversation. In D. Tannen, S. Kendall, & C. Gordon (Eds.), *Family talk: Discourse and identity in four American families* (pp. 263–282). New York: Oxford University Press.

Markus, H. R., Mullally, P. R., & Kitayama, S. (1997). Selfways: Diversity in modes of cultural participation. In U. Neisser & D. A. Jopling (Eds.), *The conceptual self in context: Culture, experience, self-understanding* (pp. 13–61). New York: Cambridge University Press.

Marsh, H. W., Smith, I. D., & Barnes, J. (1985). Multidimensional self-concepts: Relations with sex and academic achievement. *Journal of Educational Psychology, 77*(5), 581–596.

Mead, G. H. (1934). *Mind, self, and society from the standpoint of a social behaviorist.* Chicago: University of Chicago Press.

Meinong, A. (1983). *On assumptions* (J. Heanue, Ed. and Trans.). Berkeley: University of California Press. (Original work published in 1902)

Metzinger, T. (2011). The no-self alternative. In S. Gallagher (Ed.), *The Oxford handbook of the self* (pp. 279–296). New York: Oxford University Press.

Middleton, D., & Brown, S. D. (2005). *The social psychology of experience: Studies in remembering and forgetting.* London: Sage.

Miller, P. J., Mintz, J., Hoogstra, L., Fung, H., & Potts, R. (1992). The narrated self: Young children's construction of self in relation to others in conversational stories of personal experiences. *Merrill-Palmer Quarterly, 38*(1), 45–67.

Miller, P. J., Potts, R., Fung, H., Hoogstra, L., & Mintz, J. (1990). Narrative practices and the social construction of self in childhood. *American Ethnologist, 17*(2), 292–311.

Moriya, K., Mori, M., Hirasaki, Y., & Sakanoe, N. (1972). Development of self-cognition of school children: On diaries of school children. *Japanese Journal of Educational Psychology, 20*(4), 205–215. (in Japanese).

Namekawa, M. (1977). 日本作文綴方教育史1:明治篇 *(A history of sakubun and tsuzurikata education in Japan (Vol. 1), Meiji-era).* Tokyo: Kokudosha. (in Japanese).

Namekawa, M. (1978). 日本作文綴方教育史2:大正篇 *(A history of sakubun and tsuzurikata education in Japan (Vol. 2), Taisho-era).* Tokyo: Kokudosha. (in Japanese).

Namekawa, M. (1983). 日本作文綴方教育史3:昭和篇I (*A history of sakubun and tsuzurikata education in Japan (Vol. 3), Showa-era I)*. Tokyo: Kokudosha. (in Japanese).

Narita, R. (2001).「歴史」はいかに語られるか：1930年代「国民の物語」批判 (*How 'history' was narrated: A critique of 'stories of people' in the 1930s*). Tokyo: NHK Shuppan. (in Japanese)

Nelson, K. (2003). Narrative and self, myth and memory: Emergence of the cultural self. In R. Fivush & C. A. Haden (Eds.), *Autobiographical memory and the construction of a narrative self: Developmental and cultural perspectives* (pp. 3–28). Mahwah, NJ: Lawrence Erlbaum.

Nelson, K., & Fivush, R. (2004). The emergence of autobiographical memory: A social cultural developmental theory. *Psychological Review, 111*(2), 486–511.

Norrick, N. R. (2000). *Conversational narrative: Storytelling in everyday talk*. Amsterdam: John Benjamins.

Okada, A. (2009). キリストの身体:血と肉と愛の傷 (*The corpus of Christ: Blood, flesh, and wounds of love*). Tokyo: Chuo Koron Shinsha. (in Japanese).

Parker, I. (2015). *Psychology after discourse analysis: Concepts, methods, critique*. London: Routledge.

Peirce, C. S. (1892). The law of mind. *The Monist, 2*(4), 533–559.

Petrilli, S. (2013). *The self as a sign, the world, and the other*. New Brunswick, NJ: Transaction Publishers.

Piaget, J. (1955). *The construction of reality in the child* (M. Cook, Trans.). London: Routledge and Kegan Paul. (Original work published in 1937)

Piaget, J. (1985). *The equilibration of cognitive structures: The central problem of intellectual development* (T. Brown & K. J. Thampy, Trans.). Chicago: University of Chicago Press. (Original work published in 1975)

Pontecorvo, C., Fasulo, A., & Sterponi, L. (2001). Mutual apprentices: The making of parenthood and childhood in family dinner conversations. *Human Development, 44*(6), 340–361.

Potter, J., & Wetherell, M. (1987). *Discourse and social psychology: Beyond attitudes and behaviour*. London: Sage.

Preece, A. (1987). The range of narrative forms conversationally produced by young children. *Journal of Child Language, 14*(2), 353–373.

Rommetveit, R. (1985). Language acquisition as increasing linguistic structuring of experience and symbolic behavior control. In J. V. Wertsch (Ed.), *Culture, communication, and cognition: Vygotskian perspectives* (pp. 183–204). New York: Cambridge University Press.

Rommetveit, R. (1992). Outlines of a dialogically based social-cognitive approach to human cognition and communication. In A. H. Wold (Ed.), *The dialogical alternative: Towards a theory of language and mind* (pp. 19–44). Oslo: Scandinavian University Press.

Sovran, T. (1992). Between similarity and sameness. *Journal of Pragmatics, 18*(4), 329–344.

Stenner, P. (2017). *Liminality and experience: A transdisciplinary approach to the psychosocial*. London: Palgrave Macmillan.

Sugahara, M. (2016). 戦後作文・綴り方教育の史的研究 (*A historical study of sakubun and tsuzurikata education after World War II*). Hiroshima: Keisuisha. (in Japanese).

Tannen, D. (1989). *Talking voices: Repetition, dialogue, and imagery in conversational discourse*. New York: Cambridge University Press.

Toyoda, M. (1995). 新編綴方教室 (*Classes in tsuzurikata*) (M. Yamazumi, Ed.). Tokyo: Iwanami Shoten. (in Japanese) (Original work published in 1937).

Tulving, E. (1972). Episodic and semantic memory. In E. Tulving & W. Donaldson (Eds.), *Organization of Memory*. New York: Academic Press.

Turner, V. W. (1969). *The ritual process: Structure and anti-structure*. Chicago: Aldine.

Ujiie, T. (1996). 子どもは気まぐれ:ものがたる発達心理学への序章 (*Children are capricious: Introduction to developmental psychology through story*). Kyoto: Minerva Shobo. (in Japanese).

Utsumi, S. (2013). 児童養護施設の心理臨床：「虐待」のその後を生きる(*Clinical psychology in children's homes: The lives of children after abuse*). Tokyo: Nihon Hyoronsha. (in Japanese).

Valsiner, J. (2007). *Culture in minds and societies: Foundations of cultural psychology*. New Delhi: Sage.

Valsiner, J. (2017). *From methodology to methods in human psychology*. Cham: Springer International.

Valsiner, J., & van der Veer, R. (2014). Encountering the border: Vygotsky's zona blizhaishego razvitia and its implications for theories of development. In A. Yasnitsky, R. van der Veer, & M. Ferrari (Eds.), *The Cambridge handbook of cultural-historical psychology* (pp. 148–173). Cambridge, UK: Cambridge University Press.

von Ehrenfels, C. (1988a). On 'Gestalt qualities'. In B. Smith (Ed. and Trans.), *Foundations of gestalt theory* (pp. 82–117). Munich: Philosophia. (Original work published in 1890)

von Ehrenfels, C. (1988b). On Gestalt qualities. In B. Smith (Ed. and Trans.), *Foundations of gestalt theory* (pp. 121–123). Munich: Philosophia. (Original work published in 1932)

Vuorisalo, M., Raittila, R., & Rutanen, N. (2018). Kindergarten space and autonomy in construction: Explorations during team ethnography in a Finnish kindergarten. *Journal of Pedagogy, 9*(1), 45–64.

Vygotsky, L. S. (1971). *The psychology of art* (Scripta Technica, Trans.). Cambridge, MA: MIT Press.

Vygotsky, L. S. (1986). *Thought and language* (Rev. ed.) (A. Kozulin, Trans.). Cambridge, MA: MIT Press. (Original work published in 1934)

Watanabe, E. M. (2007). A comparison of language arts education in the three countries, Japan, the United States, and France: Socio historical analyses of "Reading and Writing". *Nihon-Kenkyu, 35*, 573–619. (in Japanese).

Wiley, A. R., Rose, A. J., Burger, L. K., & Miller, P. J. (1998). Constructing autonomous selves through narrative practices: A comparative study of working-class and middle-class families. *Child Development, 69*(3), 833–847.

Williams, D. (1996). *Deformed discourse: The function of the monster in mediaeval thought and literature*. Exeter, UK: University of Exeter Press.

Wimmer, H., & Perner, J. (1983). Beliefs about beliefs: Representation and constraining function of wrong beliefs in young children's understanding of deception. *Cognition, 13*(1), 103–128.

Yamamoto, M., & Komatsu, K. (2016). How fourth grade students' selves emerge in their diaries: A qualitative inquiry into the self in relation to others. *Japanese Journal of Educational Psychology, 64*(1), 76–87. (in Japanese).

Zittoun, T., & Gillespie, A. (2012). Using diaries and self-writings as data in psychological research. In E. Abbey & S. Surgan (Eds.), *Emerging methods in psychology* (pp. 1–26). New Brunswick, NJ: Transaction Publishers.

Index

© The Author(s) 2019
K. Komatsu, *Meaning-Making for Living*, SpringerBriefs in Psychology,
https://doi.org/10.1007/978-3-030-19926-5